ESPORTS IN COURT, CRIMES IN VR, AND THE 51% ATTACK

KEY TRENDS AND DEVELOPMENTS IN ESPORTS, VR AND AR, BLOCKCHAIN, AND CRYPTOCURRENCIES 2020

DAVID B. HOPPE

Esports in Court, Crimes in VR, and the 51% Attack

Key Trends and Developments in Esports, VR and AR, Blockchain, and Cryptocurrencies

2020

Contact Gamma Law:
Website: www.gammalaw.com
Email: info@gammalaw.com
Twitter: @GammaLaw
LinkedIn: http://www.linkedin.com/company/gamma-law/
Phone: +1 (415) 901-0510

SPECIAL THANKS

Special thanks to Seon King, for his thoughtful guidance and perspective, as well as to Gary Chartier for his support and friendship over many years.

CONTENTS

BLOCKCHAIN AND CRYPTOCURRENCIES

FOREWORD

Businesses across nearly all categories have become accustomed to a dizzying pace of change over the last two decades, resulting in dynamically-changing markets, rapidly-evolving consumer preferences and even the introduction of non-governmental currencies with which to purchase products and services. Much of this, of course, has been driven by the relentless development of technology and its increasing penetration of nearly every aspect of our lives, but other developments (such as the sudden appearance of esports in the mainstream consciousness) may not be so easy to explain.

And yet as established businesses have had to adapt or accept the inevitability of increasing irrelevance, the revolutionary possibilities created by new technologies and today's interconnectedness — notably blockchain, but also virtual and augmented reality (VR/AR) and even esports (a radically democratic sport with no governing organization) – bring the potential to empower individuals, undermine long-established institutions and ultimate dramatically upend society as we know it.

This book presents a snapshot of selected business, legal and societal challenges and opportunities that have arisen over the last year at the forefront of these trends, from the perspective of a California media/technology lawyer practicing in four of today's most dynamic business verticals — interactive media and esports, blockchain, digital entertainment and VR/AR. The collection of topics is deliberately serendipitous — from the new Japan esports industry organization to real-world crimes in virtual reality to blockchain and the music business — reflecting the dynamic, unpredictable nature of the processes underway to reshape our world.

Esports in Court, Crimes in VR, and the 51% Attack is above all fun, formatted in quick-read pieces and accessible to anyone with an interest in the remarkable media and technological developments underway that will affect us all.

— Naoko Okumoto
CEO & Managing Partner, Amber Bridge Partners
Palo Alto, California, January 2020

PREFACE

What do a lawsuit by a video game influencer, criminal activity in virtual worlds and a blockchain hack have in common? They're all current topics – along with many others – in the fascinating give-and-take between rapidly-developing media and technology sectors and the law (which is much less rapidly developing, in case there  was any doubt!). This book is a collection of essays, statistics and observations on a wide range of such current topics, and some thoughts on how laws may, or should, evolve in response.

The perspective is that of a San Francisco-based media and technology lawyer supporting clients in rapidly-developing business sectors, including video games and esports, virtual and augmented reality, digital media and blockchain. In each of these areas, business models seem to change on an almost-daily basis, as technologies evolve and consumer expectations shift and expand at the same rate. In this dynamic environment, today's discussion topic can be tomorrow's new opportunity or tomorrow's new threat.

Helping clients navigate these business and legal challenges and manage risk, when it's not clear whether or how current laws apply, or how courts might interpret new regulations (not to mention the extent to which they comprehend the client's business), can be a huge challenge. A deep understanding of the client's business and related challenges and opportunities – not just the law – is indispensable.

We hope you enjoy this collection of short essays and infographics, which are intended to provide a sort of serendipitous sampling of the most interesting recent topics at the cutting edge of media and technology.

– David B. Hoppe
San Francisco, California, March 2020

ESPORTS

FIVE TRENDS TO WATCH IN ESPORTS IN 2019

In this early 2019 article, we noted key business trends we expected to develop that year. The major 'hits' were the growth of mobile esports - the mobile gaming industry reached an estimated $68.5 billion in 2019, representing 45% of total gaming industry figures - and esports achieved its first $1 billion year in 2019. The trends listed in this article will continue to develop into 2020.

. . .

2019 is predicted to be the year in which the esports industry will exceed $1 billion in size. In this article, originally prepared in January, we outline five of the major trends to watch in this year of continued significant growth.

1. The Proliferation of Mobile Esports

Mobile esports have been steadily increasing in scale and popularity over recent years. In 2018, the Clash Royale League world finals offered a prize pool of $1 million, attracting over 700,000 viewers, and demonstrating that professional esports on "small screens" really can work. Moreover, continual increases in mobile technology can be expected to drive the market the greater heights. As an example, the Samsung Galaxy S10 features USB Type-C, 550ppi, an octa-core Qualcomm Snapdragon 855 processor and 8GB of RAM. These specs are high enough that an average gamer can fulfill his or her daily quota of playing without even turning on his desktop PC or gaming laptop. Also in 2018, NantWorks and Daybreak teamed up to create the mobile version of their popular PC game *H1Z1*. Other game developers like Bethesda Softworks, Blizzard, and Giant Interactive have also begun to invest resources to mobile gaming, so the best is very much yet to come.

2. Increasing Overlap with Traditional Sports

The overlap between traditional sports and esports began with sponsorships, and today teams in the NBA and NFL, a plethora of soccer clubs and traditional sports personalities such as Michael Jordan have invested in professional eSports. In 2019, the overlap will broaden to include the event level as the Southeast Asian Games (Nov 30 – Dec 11) mixes the two for the first time ever.

At the Southeast Asian Games, over fifty traditional

sports athletic events and disciplines will be held alongside a games lineup that includes Dota 2, StarCraft 2, Tekken, Arena of Valor, Mobile Legends, and more. This is history in the making and a major milestone for esports as efforts advance to make it a medals sport in an International Olympic Committee – sanctioned event.

3. The Regulation of Esports Broadcasting Rights

Copyright will become one of the foremost issues in esports in 2019. While traditional sports teams own all of their related intellectual property and associated rights, the situation for esports is markedly more complex. Game developers and publishers own the majority of associated intellectual properties and copyrights, but boundaries quickly become muddied in the case of tournaments organized by third parties. Most game developer or publishers companies do not host tournaments and third parties often fill this gap by holding esports events without the formal consent of the rights owners. Developers and publishers will continue their efforts to claim these rights for themselves.

4. Esports Reaches a New Growth Milestone

In 2018, the scale and profile of esports reached new heights. Cloud9 became the most valuable professional esports team in the world, valued at over $300 million. More than ten teams are valued above $100 million, significantly higher amounts than the year before. The main reason for the tremendous growth of esports is the entrance of non-endemic personalities and companies as significant investors in these teams. The likes of Michael Jordan, Robert Kraft, Drake and others have seen glimpses of the future and the eventual success of esports. This has brought esports and traditional sports even closer, and the first indicator is the

Roland Garros Tennis Tournament that will feature the Tennis World Tour competition alongside its main tournament. Esports events across all competitive games and continents are getting larger and more significant as investments, which means bigger tournament prize pools attracting more visitors, influential participants and other companies already investing heavily in esports. All of this in combination will result in the profile of professional esports and gaming continue to increase in 2019.

5. The Rise of Esports Schools and Scholarships

Since esports is already competing with traditional sports in every field, it is just a matter of time before universities started offering related courses, programs and scholarships for new students. The Lanxiang Technical School in China already has a program called "Esports and Management" in which they teach esports branding, event organizing, coaching and playing. The University of California has had its League of Legends program for four years now, and continues to receive support from Riot, with a new training room a d event management, among other benefits. The initial investment in gear, gaming PCs, training facilities and coaches for the team is small compared to the possible return. Prize pools in esports tournaments benefit both the University and the team of students who win it.

2

COULD THE COURTROOM BE ESPORTS' NEWEST PLATFORM?

urner 'Tfue' Tenney's groundbreaking lawsuit against his former team is still ongoing as of January 2020, with FaZe Clan filing a countersuit in New York. Tfue moved to pause the proceedings there, but the player's request was denied and the organization's lawsuit in New York continued to proceed as of November 2019. As esports is a relatively new industry, legal precedents are sparse and the potential implications for cases such as this are broad. When proceedings conclude, it may be an important reference case for future esports player contract negotiations.

· · ·

In 1956, without an agent or attorney representing him, an 18-year-old Curt Flood signed his first professional baseball contract. Twelve years later he wrote a letter to then Major League Baseball Commissioner Bowie Kuhn protesting the system that produced such contracts with onerous provisions allowing professional baseball players to be bought, sold and traded between teams as if they were property. Unsatisfied with Kuhn's response to the letter, Flood sued him in a lawsuit that would ultimately reach the United States Supreme Court.

The esports world was rocked last month after Turner "Tfue" Tenney filed a lawsuit against his former eSports team FaZe Clan, Inc in Los Angeles Superior Court. While it is somewhat of a stretch to compare this case with Flood's lawsuit against Bowie Kuhn, Tenney's suit is undergirded by many of the same employment relationship tensions which were behind Flood's suit, and it offers a glimpse at just a few of the many employment and labor related legal issues that the burgeoning esports industry will need to address if it hopes to continue to grow.

Tenney, 21 years old, joined FaZe Clan in 2018 and is presently considered one of the world's best Fortnite players. His lawsuit challenges the validity of the "Gamer Agreement" he signed with FaZe Clan, Inc. on rather narrow legal grounds. He claims the contract is unenforceable under California statutory law because FaZe Clan acted as an unlicensed talent agent and because the contract contains provisions that illegally restrict his ability to pursue his profession. FaZe Clan has claimed the contract is valid and enforceable, and has denied any wrongdoing. On the surface, the dispute highlights the need for great care to be taken in drafting esports and gaming contracts to create provisions which will stand up to court challenge if required. This should be lesson enough for esports industry interests to note. Lying just beneath the surface of the legal claims asserted by Tenney, however, are clues to a myriad of other potential labor and employment law-related issues the industry would be wise to understand exist.

Perhaps one of the most fundamental questions to be answered when determining rights and responsibilities in the employment and labor law area is the legal status of the parties involved. Is there an employer/employee relationship? Is the relationship that of an independent contractor? The Tenney lawsuit illustrates that, in the esports setting, the answer to this most basic question remains open to debate. Tenney claims that the "team" of which he was a member was acting as his agent in violating California's Talent Agency Act. This is not what would be thought of as a "typical" employer/employee relationship. The esports industry is still in its infancy and there are as yet no overall governing or organizational bodies in place. Tournament organizers range from established leagues to game developers to small volunteer or non-profit organizations. Gamers play individually or as members of "teams", some highly organized and structured, and some much less so. It remains an unanswered, and perhaps under current conditions unanswerable, as to whether gamers are employees, independent contractors, performers or athletes. This is significant because with no definitive answer the field is open for argument in any particular circumstance what the gamer's legal status is and thus how, if at all, established employment and labor law should apply to them. As a result, this leaves open for now how, if at all, eSports teams or leagues might be liable for failure to comply with such basic labor and employment laws as those found in the Fair Labor Standards Act (FLSA) or the National Labor Relations Act (NLRA) which apply only to protect employees and are not applicable to independent contractors. Organizers and teams are cautioned that incorrectly classifying as independent contractors workers who under established legal standards would be considered employees has potential legal implications and can also significantly impact the organizer's or team's ability to exercise control over the gamer's business activities or conduct.

The esports industry skews very heavily to a younger demographic. In his lawsuit, Tenney points out that he was only 20 years old when he signed the Gamer Agreement with FaZe Clan. In fact, many of the top esports gamers are below the age of 18. This means that teams, leagues and other promoters need to consider whether federal and state child labor laws and regulations are implicated by their operations. Child labor laws aside, Tenney claims that young gamers are regularly exploited by the esports entertainment companies for whom they play. He points, for example, to a "finder's fee" provision in his Gamer Agreement which he claims purportedly entitles FaZe Clan to retain up to 80% of the revenue paid by third parties for Tenney's "services". Whether it is true or not that esports organizers, leagues and teams prey unfairly upon young gamers, those active in the industry should be aware that such a perception can be created and how that perception can be exacerbated by pointing to provisions like the "finder's fee" provision in the FaZe Clan Gamer Agreement.

Curt Flood ultimately lost his legal battle with Bowie Kuhn. However, the events set in motion a decade of labor market activity during which the face of Major League Baseball was substantially changed. Players won the right to free agency. Pension contributions were escalated, and salary arbitration rights secured. Players became entitled to negotiate contracts with agent representation. Travel pay and conditions were improved among other things. It is still too early to tell what the outcome of the Tenney lawsuit against FaZe Clan will be. However, one thing of which esports organizers, leagues and teams can be certain is that this lawsuit will not be the last. As the popularity of esports continues to grow at a rapid rate and as the amount of money flowing into the industry continues to swell, all of the incentives will be in place for gamers to challenge their actions in the courts.

3

EA LEADS THE COMPETITION IN SPORTS VIDEO GAMES, SO WHY DON'T THEY LEAD IN ESPORTS?

This thought piece explores Electronic Arts' place in esports as of 2019 through a macro lens. While various factors still inhibit the company's reach, the outlook for 2020 is more favorable. Snickers has signed on as a lead sponsor of the Madden NFL 20 Club Championship thanks to the NFL, which also played a part in securing EA's Pizza Hut sponsorship.

. . .

While many video games based on traditional sports such as soccer, football, and basketball are extremely strong sellers, this has not translated into popularity as esports titles. Esports would seem to be an ideal fit for sports video games, but the most popular esports titles are multiplayer online battle-arena games (MOBAs) like *League of Legends (LoL)* and *Defense of the Ancients 2 (Dota 2)*, and first-person shooters (FPS's) such as *Counter Strike: Global Offensive (CS:GO)* and *Overwatch*. Electronic Arts (EA) is striving to develop its range of long-established and successful sports video game franchises into successful esports titles, but why haven't these games taken off as esports already?

EA's *FIFA* series of soccer video games is by far the most popular video game franchise based on a traditional sport. VentureBeat reports that 45 million unique participants played the game on PC, Xbox One, PlayStation 4, and Switch during EA's fiscal year ending March 2019. By comparison, around 100 million gamers played *League of Legends* in 2017, and RankedKings projects that number has grown to over 110 million in 2019. Moreover, average Twitch viewership for *League of Legends* content is around six times higher than that of *FIFA19*, and around 99 million viewers tuned in for the *League of Legends World Championship Finals* in 2018, while approximately 29 million viewers watched the FIFA eWorld Cup 2018 Grand Final. The prize pool for this event was $250,000, significantly below to LOL Worlds' $6.4 million. The combined prize pool for the *Dota 2* International was even higher still at $24.8 million.

Reasons for the Divide May be Experimental and Cultural

Authenticity of experience may be a major reason why traditional sports have not become popular as esports. Football, basketball, and soccer all have real world equivalents with real athletes, real life drama and competition, and fans often have strong emotional attachments to their favorite players and teams. Video games and the resulting competitions are limited, virtual reproductions, with all the shortfalls that may come with that. Conversely, in the case of games like *LoL* and *Dota 2*, the video games *are* the authentic experience, and competition can be no more authentic or emotionally charged than high-level esports.

There have been cases of fans pushing back against traditional sports crossing over into video games: these sports fans worry that esports versions of their favorite sport will erode its value. For example, Forbes reports that, in September of 2018, *"a Swiss Super League Soccer match had to be halted because fans threw game console controllers onto the pitch in opposition to a proposed official Swiss esports league. They believe club resources should be focused solely on soccer, not a commercial venture that could threaten tradition."*

EA Sports is "in the Game"

Electronic Arts is the leading publisher of sports-based video games, and its popular sports franchises *FIFA*, *Madden NFL*, and *NBA Live*. Of these, soccer is the most popular global sport, and *FIFA* is EA's most popular sports series and potentially the best-poised for success in esports competition.

While the popularity of *FIFA* esports has yet to reach the levels of the leading MOBA or FPS titles, EA is making significant investments and efforts to promote and grow the scene. Some 300 to 400 EA staff work on esports, according to Todd Sitrin, senior VP and general manager of EA's competitive gaming division. EA's competitive gaming division has around 30 partners, including tournament operator Gfinity, esports league PGL, and a host of real-world soccer leagues including the English Premier League, La Liga, League One,

The Dutch League, and MLS in North America. Fifteen to twenty leagues run licensed competitions in partnership with EA. As a result of these efforts, the total viewership numbers for competitive *FIFA* tripled last year, and about 20 million people competed at the beginning of the *FIFA eWorld Cup* qualifiers.

Speaking to the perceived threat that soccer esports may present to traditional soccer, the English Premier League's Managing Director, Richard Masters, told Forbes that *"there is a desire to ensure that the overall product is not threatened by the rise of competitive gaming and to ensure it continues to attract the attention of younger audiences."*

In addition to *FIFA* esports, EA also created the Madden NFL Championship Series (MCS), which features a series of qualifying events, open tournaments, and a major championship event called the *Madden Bowl*. Similarly, the EA Sports NHL 18 tournament gives hockey esports fans and competitors an opportunity to win a championship trophy and their share of a $100,000 prize pool.

Prospects for Growth

EA believes that its sports-based video games franchises have the potential to compete with *LoL*, *Dota 2*, and *CS:GO* as esports, and justifiably so. Given their accessibility and fandoms that reach into the billions, traditional sports still have a great deal of untapped potential to realize as esports, provided that the divide between real sports fandom and esports fandom can be bridged.

Esports and the majority of its viewers are still young. Future generations will grow up with esports, entrenched attitudes will evolve, and so significant increases in viewership and participation are arguably inevitable. Emerging technologies may also prove to be a catalyst for growth for sports video games esports. In an interview with VentureBeat, Matt Bilbey, EA's executive VP for strategic growth, said that the company is working on developing AR and VR for games like *FIFA19*: *"whether it's AR on a table in front of you, where you see a stadium render, whether you're playing or just watching the eWorld Cup final, I think there are definitely options that will bring even closer engagement to what's happening on the pitch."*

While esports based on traditional sports presently lags esports based on other genres, the potential for them to catch up and achieve sizeable market share is undeniable, and EA seems both determined and poised to realize and capture this opportunity.

4

MOBILE SPORTS' EAST-WEST DIVIDE

W hile the concentration of mobile esports still skews toward countries in the East, there are signs for significant potential growth in the West over 2020. The developers of PUBG Mobile have devoted $5 million to overhauling their global tournament structure, and Clash Royale is teaming up with Turner Sports to oversee ad inventory. In addition, Riot Games will be releasing Legends: Wild Rift, which likely to garner attention from players in every region. A rightening of the balance between East and West mobile esports can be only a matter of time.

. . .

While mobile esports are hugely popular in Asia, western esports have been largely divided into PC and console camps. Recently this has begun to change, and the mobile esports scenes in North America and Europe have begun to increase in popularity. In spite of this relatively late start, there are signs that mobile esports may yet gain ground in the West .

"Mobile First" Culture Sets the Ground for Mobile Esports in Asia

The primary reason for this difference in esports platform preferences between Asia and the West is what has been dubbed Asia's "mobile-first culture". Reasons for this include average housing sizes in Asia being smaller than in the west, which means less space for personal computer setups; widely available public transportation and commutes that are on average longer than Western countries greatly facilitating the use of mobile devices while on the move; and widely available access to strong 4G, LTE and broadband/wifi connections. A recent whitepaper by gaming and esports industry researchers Newzoo say that the "mobile-first" trend originated in Japan, which drove mobile technology and the proliferation of mobile devices domestically and in Asia from the early 2000s. Now, mobile devices are the first point of entry to the internet for up to 90% of users in Asia, and China is currently the world's largest mobile market. Once smartphones superseded non-smart devices and, together with tablets, became increasingly powerful, gaming experiences that were previously the sole domain of PC and consoles could be replicated on mobile devices, and the stage was set for mobile esports to succeed in the region.

According to a recent Akamai report, *"mobile devices are the preferred platform to watch and participate in esports"* in North Asia. The 2018 Asian games provide one example of the Asia's commitment to mobile esports: the event included esports as a demonstration sport, and two of the five titles played were mobile esports: Arena of Valor and Clash Royale. China and Indonesia took the gold in those titles, respectively. Tournament prize pools provide another insight into the importance of mobile esports in the region: the 2018 prize pool for China's Clash Royal league was $40,000, and an Arena of Valor "international league" offered a $600,000 prize pool. The entire proceeds of the latter were won by Asian teams.

The West is Behind, But Shows Potential

While North American and European teams also participate in these international tournaments, they do so in disproportionately smaller numbers than their Asian counterparts. Mobile esports have been slow to catch on in the West partially due to entirely different mobile cultures in the two regions. While smartphones and tablets are popular in Western countries, they primarily serve the purposes of consumption of content and of communication, and are generally eschewed for the more powerful platforms for the purposes of participating in esports. As Newzoo's report forecasts, *"PC is still the dominant form of gaming entertainment in the West and is expected to remain so for the coming years. While mobile has quickly grown as the biggest gaming screen worldwide, its esports scene still lags behind that of PC as well as console."*

Just the same, mobile esports are expected to continue to grow in the West. Dreamhack recently concluded its first Dreamhack Mobile Series event, which featured Clash Royale and Brawl Stars and a prize pool of $20,000. Collegiate leagues have also experimented with mobile tournaments: Vainglory was hosted by Collegiate Starleague in 2017-2018, and showcased at popular events including PAX East and TwitchCon. The popularity of mobile esports in Asia market may prove to be a driver of growth in the West, as qualifiers in professional mobile esports in the West often feed into larger international tournaments held by companies such as Tencent or Supercell. Recently ESL teamed up with Supercell to announce a $1 million tournament for Clash of Clans in Europe and North America. In another developing trend, YouTube is hosting higher numbers of mobile game streamers than Twitch.

The Future of Esports May Well be Mobile

Esports is still a young industry and in many ways still in the early stages of development. While the balance of popularity of mobile esports between Asia and the West is presently very uneven, the future may look very different. Mobile gaming is predicted to account for an increasingly larger share of the overall games market in future, and Newzoo predicts that 50% of games purchased will be played on mobile devices by 2020. Given this, the sheer ubiquity of mobile platforms, and continued investment and promotion by developers, publishers, and event organizers, mobile esports have the potential to bridge the gap between East and West, and perhaps even one day become the mainstay of the industry worldwide.

AN OUNCE OF MEDICINE: IN LIEU OF REGULATION, IT FALLS TO ESPORTS ATHLETES TO SEEK EARLY LEGAL SUPPORT

The ongoing lawsuit between Turner 'Tfue' Tenney and FaZe Clan vividly illustrates how the adage that 'an ounce of prevention is still worth a pound of cure' still holds true. Esports legal precedents are slowly becoming established by cases such as this and more recent cases such as former NBA player Rick Fox's suing of partners for misappropriation of funds and Cloud9's issue relating to tournament rules. Esports law is yet to become established in many areas where traditional sports are strong, and for this reason it is important to have counsel when entering negotiations as the industry matures.

. . .

All new industries experience growing pains, and problems arising from legal issues are particularly common. In many cases, the legal learning curve broadly follows those of similar businesses and industries; the still young esports industry is already dealing with many issues that plague established sports, but the situation is complicated by the lack of any dominant governing body or standardized regulations.

The esports industry today is worth $1 billion, the top five esports games pay out over =$400 million in prizes, and top tier esports athletes can earn millions of dollars. With this much money at stake and so little oversight or regulation, high-earning esports players require adequate representation now more than ever.

The requirement for legal protection has been high-lighted by a number of cases in recent weeks. At the time of writing, a former coach has filed a suit against NRG Esports for unpaid salary; Team Secret settled a payment dispute and reshuffled its management team after players claimed they were owed their tournament winnings; Korea's top Overwatch team recently complained of poor living conditions and abuse from their management, and Turner 'Tfue' Tenney recently sued team FaZe Clan claiming that his contract with them is overly oppressive, unconscionable, and blatantly unfair.

A number of organizations have begun efforts to implement standardized regulations, such as the Esports Integrity Coalition, which has created a code of ethics, procedures to promote fairness, reporting requirements, and a list of known cheaters. A number of player associations such as NALCSPA have been established to ensure fair contracts for their members. Laudable as these efforts are, they are still in their infancy in terms of reach and efficacy, and the fragmented nature of the approaches means inconsistent application.

Presently, only a small percentage of players are represented by an attorney or a professional manager, and many of the athletes are very young. In most cases, young players do not have the experience to fully understand the provisions and implications of contracts, making the need for the support of an attorney or manager even greater.

To avoid potential contract disputes, it is critical that players engage attorneys early in contract discussions. A whole host of potential legal issues can be avoided with sufficient advance diligence. Having an attorney review and negotiate contracts can go a long way toward ensuring a level playing field. Moreover, experienced legal professionals who are familiar with esports contracts, industry standards, and potentially lucrative areas of opportunity such as streaming, sponsorship, and licensing has a much greater chance of negotiating better esports contracts for players.

Esports is still young, developing, and fraught with potential pitfalls for all industry actors, not least the players. Until governing entities and standardized regulations are put in place to protect esports athletes from issues such as unfair contracts and playing conditions, the only parties looking out for the players are the players themselves, and support from experienced professionals is critical.

A COMMUNITY SUCCESS STORY: DOTA 2'S 'THE INTERNATIONAL' BREAKS FORTNITE'S RECORD FOR BIGGEST TOURNAMENT PRIZE POOL

hile The International was able to beat Fortnite's record for biggest single tournament prize pool of 2019, the year ended with Fortnite substantially ahead of Dota 2 with regard to total prize money. Epic Games awarded $64.42 million compared to Valve's $41.4 million, largely as part of that year's marketing campaign behind Fortnite. Given that The International's prize pool is highly dependent upon crowdfunding and that Dota 2's player base is showing signs of contraction, Fortnite may well be the overall winner for 2020.

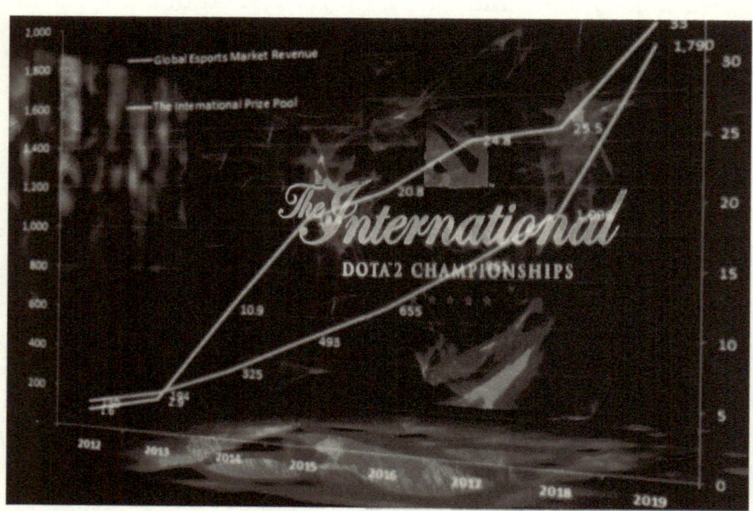

. . .

This summer, the annual Dota 2 world championship esports tournament, 'The Invitational', has once again made headlines for a record-breaking prize pool. In its ninth year, the Dota 2 championship pot has grown to $33.4 million. The figure alone is newsworthy for beating the recent $30 million Fortnite World Cup purse, but has further significance because it makes TI9 the biggest payout for a single esports event to date, and because the majority of the prize pool was accumulated through crowdfunding.

The International's prize pools have included a crowdfunded component since TI3, which was held in 2013. Ahead of TI3, the first 'Compendium', an interactive booklet that tracks tournament statistics and usually includes tournament tickets, was launched and a portion of its sales was allocated to The International's prize pool. Together with Valve's fixed prize pool contribution of $1,600,000, proceeds from compendium sales grew the TI3 prize pool to $2.9 million.

Every year since then, the range of Dota 2-related products that contribute to the prize pool has grown to include battle passes and other in-game items, and incentives have become increasingly attractive to players. By 2018, the crowdfunded portion of the prize pool had grown to almost fifteen times the size of Valve's fixed base contribution. Last year's TI8 broke the standing record for prize pool by raising $25.5 million in crowdfunding, almost a million dollars more than the previous year's event, before being surpassed by the Fortnite World Cup Purse in July 2019.

This year, players can purchase the base battle pass for $9.99, run the challenges in it, and opt to invest again for more leveling options. While funds from battle passes for other games such as Apex Legends generally go entirely to the publisher, 25 percent of the revenue from sales of selected Dota 2 items goes to the championship pot, well into the event season. As a result, players are able to actively contribute to the success of The International, which goes a long way to keeping the players and audience engaged over the year-long circuit.

As a result of player contributions, The International holds six of the top ten largest prize pools in esports history. Epic Games' 2019 Fortnite event now holds second place, and Riot Games rounds out the lower three spots, with the largest of their prize pools being $6.4 million for League of Legends Worlds in 2018. Moreover, annual growth of The International's prize pool has outperformed the growth of global esports market revenue, as illustrated below.

Global Esports Market Revenue vs The International Prize Pool

Source: bitinfocharts.com

One might expect that the steady growth of the event's prize pool would correlate with an increase in the popularity of Dota 2, but this has not been the case. The August 2019 player base for Dota 2 was 452,726 players, but peak player base was reached over three years ago when 709,103 players logged on in February 2016. The growth of prize money has been a result of the support of the solid player base of 500,000 or so and the effective development, promotion, and sales by Valve of the Compendiums, battle passes, and other in-game items that support the prize pool.

How long Valve and the Dota 2 community can maintain the growth of The International and its prize pool is anyone's guess, but the longevity and exceptional success of the funding model has already led some other developers and publishers to follow suit, for example the Smite World Championship and recently the League of Legends World Championship. At present, however, the Fortnite World Cup Finals is the only other tournament that has exceeded $10 million in prize money, so competition is at present limited and for now The International reigns supreme.

THE REMARKABLE SUCCESS OF THE JAPANESE ESPORTS UNION (JESU)

The boom in Japanese esports ignited by the efforts of JeSU continue has not been without hiccups. As one notable example, popular Street Fighter V player Yusuke Momochi refused to apply for a player license with the organization out of protest, and as a result was unable to receive the full prize amount of Capcom Pro Tour's Asia Premier. The tide, however, is very much in JeSU's favor, and continued expansion and achievements are expected for the JeSU and the Japanese esports industry over 2020.

. . .

In spite of Japan being one of the world's leading video game markets, prior to early last year, the development Japan's esports scene was severely restricted due to centuries-old gambling legislation that effectively banned the offering of prize money in tournaments. In February of 2018, the Japanese esports Union (JeSU), a coalition of game publishers and other companies involved in esports, was formed to promote and represent this new industry. Eighteen months later, JeSU has successfully brought about significant developments in government regulation and popular perception that have unfettered Japanese esports and help to launch dramatic growth of the industry.

Consolidation Is Key

JeSU was formed by the combination of three independent esports associations: the Japan eSports Association, the eSports Promotion Organization, and the Japan eSports Federation. The formation of the union was supported by the Computer Entertainment Suppliers Association (CESA), which exists to promote the video game industry and organizes Tokyo Game Show, the Japan Online Game Association (JOGA), Japan Amusement Machine and Marketing Association (JAMMA), and Association of Media in Digital (AMD). JeSU's roster of 42 regular members is comprised of Japanese video games publishers, developers and related companies of every scale and includes Arc System Works, Bandai Namco, Capcom, Dentsu, Konami, Microsoft Japan, Shogakukan, Sony, Square Enix and Tencent Japan.

Overcoming Challenges

Japanese legislation includes decades-old gambling laws that were originally established to restrict organized crime (*yakuza*), but had been interpreted to prevent esports tournaments from offering cash prizes over 100,000 yen ($934), and so limited development of the esports scene. One of JeSU's earliest accomplishments was to develop a way to work around these laws by instituting categories of "Pro Gaming" licenses which permit holders to compete in tournaments for cash prizes. The types of licenses available are the "Japan eSports Pro Licenses", the "Japan eSports Junior License", and the "Japan eSports Team License".

The introduction of licenses both enabled the offering of cash prizes in tournaments and opened the door to Japanese video game players and teams seeking to make careers in esports. To date, JeSU has issued 138 pro player licenses, one junior license, and eight team licenses across a lineup of eleven games that includes *Street Fighter V Arcade Edition, Tekken 7, Call of Duty Black Ops,* and *Puyo Puyo.*

Capturing Hearts and Minds

In addition to introduction of legislative measures, JeSU is also bringing about a cultural shift. *"In order to raise the cognition and status of [pro gamers], we thought that we needed an item that can make the pro gamer accepted by everyone,"* said Akihito Furusawa, the auditor of Japan esports Federation. JeSU work to promote and bring credibility to esports to the Japanese public. As the Japan Times reported in May 2019, *"a Jiji Press survey showed that 42.8 percent of people think esports competitive video games will become as popular as sports in Japan, up 7.4 percentage points from the previous survey carried out in April last year."*

JeSU also organizes and provides official support for esports events on a near-monthly basis. In 2019 alone, the organization has supported five events including the Puyo Puyo Championship Cup and the Tekken 7 event Wellplayed Challenger; earlier this month held the inaugural Coca-Cola

STAGE: 0 eSPORTS High School Championship 2019 which included *League of Legends*, *Fortnite,* and *Clash Royale* tournaments, and was broadcast on several national and local TV stations.

JeSU further plans to hold an exhibition event at the 2020 Tokyo Olympics and to create regional branches across the country which will support organizing esports tournaments and the training and development of local eAthletes. Additionally, the organization plans to expand opportunities for current professional Japanese eAthletes by sending them abroad for international tournaments and by organizing matches with overseas players. JeSU is well on the way to creating a foundation for Japanese teams to compete in the 2022 Asian Games in Hangzhou, China, where esports may be a full medal event for the first time.

A Burgeoning Market and Bright Outlook

The results of JeSU's efforts have been dramatic: according to the Japanese data provider Gzbrain, the Japanese esports industry grew 1244% from $3.4 million in 2017 to $42.3 million in 2018, and is predicted to growth to $90.8 million USD by 2022. Thanks to JeSU, Japan is now one of the fastest-growing esports markets in the world, and the organization is putting significant plans in place for the remainder of 2019 and beyond.

As increasing numbers of Japanese players and leagues gain new professional status and the cultural perceptions surrounding esports gradually shifts, continued and significant development and growth is forecast for this market, and Japan is already on the way to playing an important role in the global esports industry.

INFOGRAPHIC: ESPORTS IN JAPAN 2019

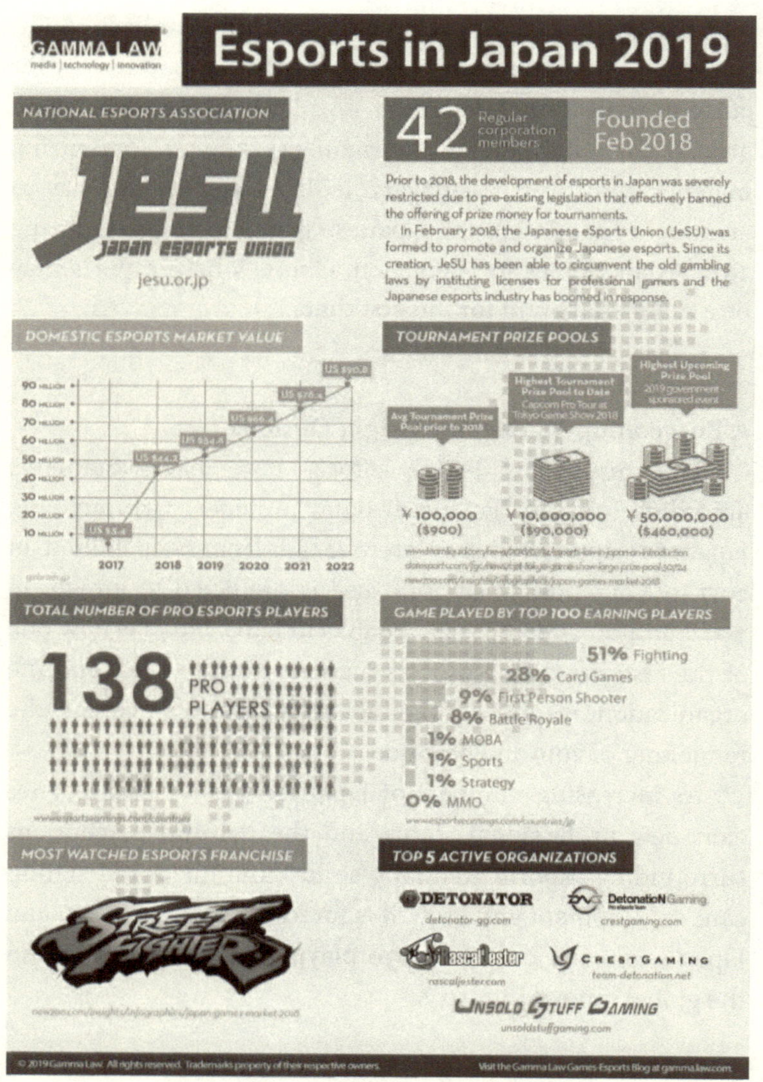

https://gammalaw.com/j-esports/

WHY THE NCAA SIDESTEPPED
COLLEGIATE ESPORTS (FOR NOW)

The NCAA's exploratory missions into the esports space and have so far concluded that it should not make a landing just yet. While we await the arguably inevitable breaking of this frontier, the NCAA has lifted the restriction on student athletes profiting from their name, image and likeness in traditional collegiate sports. Assuming that the NCAA will become involved in esports, this is a very welcome development for esports players, the majority of whom generate significant portions of their income through activities outside of tournament.

. . .

North American collegiate esports is growing at a rapid pace. Five years ago, the scene was comprised of just a small number of trailblazers, but today over 100 schools field varsity teams play for scholarships and valuable screen time on outlets like Twitch and ESPN. However, after months of evaluating the space and to the surprise of many, the NCAA announced in May that it had voted not to take a role as the governing authority for college esports leagues.

The NCAA's reluctance to commit to esports became evident in January, when NCAA president Mark Emmett expressed immediate concerns about the content of games that are played in the collegiate leagues: *"We know a lot of the content is hugely misogynistic,"* he said, *"We know that some of the content is really violent. We don't particularly embrace games where the objective is to blow your opponent's head off. We know there are serious concerns about health and wellness around those games."*

While appropriateness of content would seem to be the ostensible reason for NCAA's decision, perhaps more significant obstacles to its involvement can be found in 'Title IX' and complications from IP ownership.

In order to qualify for federal funding, college sports must abide by the rules laid out in the Title IX of the Education Amendments Act of 1972. Per Title IX, *"No person in the United States shall, on the basis of sex, be excluded from participation in, be denied the benefits of, or be subjected to discrimination under any education program or activity receiving Federal financial assistance."* At present, the ratio of male-to-female collegiate esports players is heavily male-skewed.

Low levels of female participation in collegiate esports may be due to low demand, or alternatively due to collegiate programs being allegedly inadequately accessible to female players. The latter would provide the NCAA significant reason to demur. At present, it is difficult to gauge how equitably each college recruits for esports teams due to the very limited number of successful long-term programs, but data available in the wider market does little to suggest a gender-balanced field. While the ratio is changing, esports is vastly more popular among males than females, and as such, demand from males for esports scholarships is much higher, and schools struggle to assemble co-ed esports teams.

Abiding by Title IX for traditional sports on campus generally requires that colleges offer male and female team options in proportion to attendance levels at the school. This is the reason that there are men's basketball and women's basketball divisions in the NCAA. Presently, few professional esports offer male and female leagues on the basis that gender does not affect performance in video games. On the collegiate level, so far only Stephens College in Missouri has assembled an all-female scholarship esports team, and the team has yet to play in co-ed leagues.

IP ownership poses another significant hurdle for the NCAA. Unlike traditional sports which are based on "free use" games, the rights to esports titles are held by the developers and publishers that create them and control how the games are used in competitive settings. Riot Games and Blizzard Entertainment have developed their own 'in-house' college programs, called the Riot Scholastic Association of America and Tespa, respectively. These companies run the premier tournaments for League of Legends, Overwatch, Hearthstone, and StarCraft, awarding scholarships as prizes. Other organizations such as Collegiate Starleague and AVGL offer independent leagues and prizes for games that are not managed by the developers themselves, such as Data 2, Smash Bros, and Counterstrike. This makes for complex ownership situations that are difficult to navigate and enforce top-down supervision, especially for an organization which is relatively new to the scene, as is the case with NCAA.

The reaction from students has been generally favorable. NCAA scholarship athletes are unable to receive revenue from sponsorships and tournament winnings, an issue which has been the subject of heavy debate over the years. Many college-aged esports athletes already maintain their own streams and partnerships that benefit them financially; these would likely have to be terminated should the existing North American collegiate model to applied to esports.

The major benefit to derive from the participation of the NCAA would an advocating organization that could help standardize campus esports. Many school teams such as Western University of Ontario are not officially supported by their universities; in fact, more student-run esports college organizations exist today than scholarship programs.

Should the NCAA enter the collegiate esports, it could lobby for institutional support on behalf of smaller club programs. Communication and relationships between schools, developers, and leagues would be smoothed out by necessity, and a more inclusive environment for male and female gamers could be fostered.

While it may have elected not to participate for now, it is highly likely that this decision will be revisited and reassessed in the future. In the meantime, the absence of the NCAA will provide other actors across and around the esports industry an opportunity to chart the future of collegiate esports.

10

ESPORTS INVESTMENT OPPORTUNITIES ARE ON THE RISE. HERE ARE KEY STOCKS AND ETFS TO WATCH

In addition to the developer-centric stocks and ETFs listed in this October 2019 article, there are other notable potential investments on the broadcast, entertainment, and hardware sides of esports. These include China's two biggest streaming platforms, Huya (HUYA) and Douyu (DOYU), the Sweden-based Modern Times Group (MTGB SS) which focuses on esports and gaming entertainment and holds large stakes in events production companies ESL and Dreamhack, and the gaming hardware maker Razer (1337.HK) which sponsors a variety of esports brands.

· · ·

As esports continues to grow, so do opportunities to invest in the business. Investors seeking to profit from this period of exponential growth have a variety of stocks and exchange-traded funds (ETFs) covering various segments within the esports industry from which to choose.

Esports Stocks

The games underlying the leagues, tournaments, and events around the globe are at the core of the esports industry and so the stocks of their developers and publishers are obvious considerations for equity investment. So too are the hardware manufacturers that both drive and benefit from advancement in the video games industry, as their processors, microchips and other equipment form a key part of the technological foundation that supports such gaming.

Activision Blizzard Inc.

If a gaming company is measured by the success of the games it produces, Activision Blizzard (NASDAQ: ATVI) would certainly be considered an industry success. The company's flagship game, Overwatch, is one of the principal esports games, having spawned numerous leagues and competitions that have helped grow its reach and popularity.

Activision previously agreed to a two-year, $90 million deal with Twitch to distribute the first two seasons of Overwatch League in North America. This partnership has helped grow the Overwatch brand and reach throughout the esports world. Due to its success, the Overwatch League has garnered major sponsorship partners, which include Coca-Cola Co., Toyota Motor Corp., T-Mobile US Inc., HP Inc. and Intel Corp.

Activision recently hired its first CMO, David Messinger, a veteran of Creative Artists Agency (CAA) and there have recently been talks of Disney acquiring the company as Disney looks to expand its reach in the entertainment industry.

Electronic Arts Inc.

Electronic Arts (NASDAQ: EA) is a pillar of the global video games industry and has been developing and publishing games since the 1980s.

Over the years, EA has come to prioritize multiplayer games, many of which are well-suited to esports. One of EA's key differentiating resources is its well-established line of EA Sports titles, many of which are based upon exclusive license deals with major sports brands and professional leagues, and includes FIFA, Madden NFL, NHL, NBA Live, and UFC. Of these, the FIFA series is one of the biggest global franchises, far surpassing any other sports titles in terms of Twitch viewership, and EA Sports Madden, which has been a dominant title in sports gaming for decades, and shows no signs of slowing down, with a record number of pre-sales for Madden 2020 in August 2019.

EA's most recent quarterly results showed an increase in revenue without any new game releases. This seems to indicate that EA can continue to build its business on its already solid foundation of games, and if future releases have the same staying power, it would seem that EA's business would continue to grow.

Tencent Holdings Ltd.

China-based Tencent Holdings (OTC: TCHEY) operates in an array of internet-based services, from entertainment to artificial intelligence. On the esports front, Tencent is now the parent company of Riot Games, the US video game developer. Riot of course is developer of League of Legends (LOL), a global sensation that has resulted in esports leagues and competitions around the globe. Last year, LOL fans logged a total of 10.65 million viewing hours watching the game's eight-day world championship tournament.

Tencent also holds a minority stake in Epic Games, creator of Gears of War, Infinity Blade, and Fortnite, which has a base of 250 million registered users. It should be noted, however, that even after the highly-touted Fortnite world championship with a $3 million first-place prize, the game has been on a steady decline, and is losing users and revenue after bringing in $2.4 billion in revenue last year.

As Fortnite tries to regain its footing, Tencent has begun to build its esports portfolio on its own. The company is developing new games itself which it hopes it can add to its portfolio of esports successes.

With a market cap of some $429 billion and a portfolio of household gaming names, Tencent is one of the world's largest gaming and social media companies. An investment in Tencent is a bet on popular games like League of Legends and Fortnite, while also a stake in an innovative international conglomerate with its sights set on much more than the esports industry.

Nintendo Co. Ltd.

Nintendo (OTC: NTDOY) has been a household name for decades, even for those who aren't familiar with esports culture. With a market cap of $44.6 billion, the company occupies a central place in the video games economy and esports as well.

Though Nintendo was slow to enter the esports market, *Super Smash Bros.* has long been a staple of fighting game tournaments. Recently the company announced two official esports tournaments for 2019 in Japan for *Splatoon*

2 and *Super Smash Bros. Ultimate.* And recently CBS agreed to air the Nintendo World Championships later this year.

Nintendo continues to iterate on its popular games and consoles. Nintendo's newest console, the Nintendo Switch, has already sold almost 37 million units to date. A newer, cheaper version of the Switch will be released later in 2019, as Nintendo hopes to bring in even more users that it previously was not able to attract.

Nintendo also partnered with Tencent to bring the Switch to the Chinese market, with Tencent providing server and cloud services for the console's online platform. Partnerships such as these may contribute to further growth of the company's brand and position in the global esports market.

Nvidia Corp.

Growth of major chip and system designer Nvidia (NAS-DAQ: NVDA) has been boosted by a demand for its products in the esports and video games industries. Graphic processing units (GPUs) have been especially popular for gamers looking to improve the quality of experience an competitiveness.

To solidify itself in the esports world, Nvidia has entered sponsorship arrangements across the industry, with its GPU brand GeForce supporting a variety of esports teams.

Nvidia's stock price took a major hit in 2018, as the cryptocurrency prices dropped and demand for Nvidia hardware used in cryptocurrency mining fell dramatically. Even with such a decrease in demand, sales of its GPUs seems to have stabilized.

With strong fundamentals and a solid position in the esports industry by way of sponsorships and its highly sought-after GPUs, Nvidia seems set to maintain and strengthen its market-leading position.

. . .

Esports Exchange Traded Funds

Investing in an esports ETF is akin to making an investment in the success of the esports industry as a whole. In spite of the youth of the esports industry, a number of esports ETFs are currently available. While volume is relatively low for each ETF, it seems likely that this will change as the scale and profile of the esports industry continue to grow.

ESPO

VanEck's Vectors Video Gaming and esports ETF, known as ESPO, was the first single, tradable ETF to bundle stocks from across the esports industry. ESPO began public trading on October 16, 2018 and is comprised of companies that derive over 50% of revenues from the video gaming and/or esports industry. These companies have market caps in excess of $150 million, have a three-month average daily turnover greater than $1 million, and a minimum trading volume of 250,000 shares each month over the preceding six months.

Major holdings of ESPO include all of the companies previously mentioned as Advanced Micro Devices (NASDAQ: AMD) and Take-Two Interactive Software Inc. (NASDAQ: TTWO) among others.

NERD

Created by a firm called Roundhill Investments, the NERD ETF launched on June 4, 2019 on the NYSE. It is based on the Roundhill BITKRAFT esports Index (NERD Index) and tracks the esports industry based upon the combined performance of 25 companies including video game publishers, streaming networks, esports tournament and league operators/owners, competitive team owners, and hardware companies.

Top holdings include Sea Ltd. (SE), Modern Times Group MTG AB (MTGB SS), Activision Blizzard Inc. (ATVI), HUYA Inc (HUYA), and Take-Two Interactive Software (TTWO).

HERO

The esports ETF HERO launched on the Toronto Stock Exchange (TSX) on June 17, 2019 by Canadian firm Evolve. The fund's investment objective is to replicate the performance of the Solactive eGaming Index, created by the German index firm.

With a starting AUM of $1 million and a NAV of $20, this ETF includes companies like Sony Corp. (SNE), Nintendo Ltd. (NTDOY), Activision Blizzard Inc. (ATVI), Tencent Holdings Ltd. (TCEHY), iShares MSCI South Korea ETF (EWY), NetEase Inc. (NTES), Electronic Arts Inc. (EA), and Sea Ltd. (SE). The fund's focus is on Asian and North American companies, especially those in Japan, China, and the United States.

11

NINTENDO'S 'COMPLICATED' RELATIONSHIP WITH ESPORTS

intendo's stance on esports is unique for a company that develops one of the most popular competitive titles in the world, Super Smash Brothers. Since we published this piece, Nintendo has doubled down on their view of the place of tournament prize winnings. Nintendo president Shuntaro Furukawa recently stated that there is no need for "antagonism" in their ecosystem: "In order to make our company's games be played by a broad range of people, regardless of experience, gender, or generation, we also want to make our events joinable by a broad range of people. Being able to have a different world view from other companies – without a large sum of prize money – is our strength."

Nintendo, producer of the world's most popular video games console and one of the most popular esports titles, has historically avoided positively engaging with esports, and only recently begun to participate in growing competitive gaming scene. Late though it may be, this change may very well be the tipping point from which Nintendo assumes a leading role on the stage of global esports.

Grassroots Support

Nintendo has indirectly been part of the esports scene since the release of Super Smash Bros. Melee for GameCube in 2001. Following the release of the game, dedicated Super Smash Bros. players built an independent competitive scene with no support and little recognition from Nintendo. Small local and regional Melee LAN tournaments led to a notable position in the Major League Gaming circuit over 2003 to 2006, and each year an increasingly substantial scene expanded across North America. Even after MLG dropped the title, players continued to compete at Melee in tournaments such as Evo and Genesis, attesting to the power of the game as a competitive title, which is largely due to the level of mastery required to become a successful player.

Nintendo's Heel Turn

Nintendo's evolving response to the popularity of Super Smash Bros. in esports moved from ambivalence to open hostility when it banned MLG from live streaming Brawl matches during its 2010 Pro Circuit. MLG was unable to obtain the rights to stream or VOD capture the game's content, and the only way fans could see the tournament was in person. Melee made a comeback in 2013 as a featured tournament title at Evo, but not before Nintendo once again attempted to ban any live streaming of the game. Evo's organizers even claimed that the company tried to remove the tournament from Evo altogether. Nintendo's eventual relenting in this case seemed to mark a shift in its attitude to esports.

More Power to the People

The 2013 documentary "The Smash Brothers" gives a rich history of the height of Melee's popularity, profiling some of the top players during the mid-to-late 2000s. Despite skirting direct categorization of Super Smash Bros. as an 'esports' title, the film's success reinvigorated the popularity of the franchise during what was a the beginning of a major growth period for esports, and raised expectations that Nintendo would finally engage with the scene.

Making Peace

The next iteration of the franchise for 3DS and Wii U came out in 2014 and Nintendo surprised by hosting an invitational tournament at E3 that year that featured 16 top professional players from the Melee, Brawl, and Project M scenes. To many this felt like an olive branch extended to the competitive community; approval and excitement could be seen by the fact that Smash became the most tweeted-about topic at E3. However, there was little to no follow up by Nintendo after this invitational, and the operation of Smash tournaments was once again relegated to independent tournament organizers.

Nintendo 'Switches' Gears ...?

Many believed that Nintendo's toward esports would finally turn the corner when the Nintendo Switch launched in 2017. Splatoon 2, which launched in July 2017, was the first esports-friendly title released on the new system. Prior to the game going on sale, Nintendo hosted a World Inkling Invitational at E3, further fuelling the hopes and expectations of the esports community. However, there would be no other Nintendo-sponsored tournaments until the World Cup event at E3 in 2018, which featured only an invitational qualifier. It would be another year until Nintendo announced an official competitive Splatoon platform to search for professional teams and hosted events. Unfortunately, this feature is currently only available outside of North America, so denying access for a large section of players.

Raising Expectations

It would take the next Smash title, Super Smash Bros. Ultimate, to truly inspire hope in the community that Nintendo would support building an esports scene. Marketing for the game actually seemed geared towards an esports audience, and the portability of the Switch would naturally lean to easy competitive setups at events and even online. To display the full functionality of the game before release in late 2018, Nintendo hosted another (non-monetary prize) invitational at E3. Response to the gameplay and mechanics were largely positive, more so than Super Smash Bros. Brawl or Super Smash Bros. 4, indicating that the developers had knowingly created a strong foundation for a competitive scene. Nintendo seemed to warm up even more to esports by 2019, hosting officially sanctioned tournaments for Smash Ultimate and Splatoon 2 leading up to Pax East.

·   ·   ·

Positive Developments

2019 may be a true turning point for Nintendo's relationship with esports. Nintendo recently announced a port of Blizzard's Overwatch title, which seems to be a case of a developer going all-in on developing an esports infrastructure. While this does not mean that the Switch will become a competitive platform for Overwatch, it will join titles like Fortnite, ARMS and Rocket League on the system as options for esports-driven multiplayer games on the console.

In another interesting twist, Nintendo UK recently announced a partnership with Digital Schoolhouse to bring the Switch to classrooms. A part of the deal will bring a sanctioned Smash Ultimate team battle tournament across 60 schools, reaching over 60,000 students. The intention of this program is to "foster the development of skillsets" in students for a computer-learning future. It also conveniently places Nintendo again as a tournament organizer, this time on the growing high school and collegiate level.

Conservative Heads May Prevail in the Short Term

However, even with these positive developments, it is important to recognize Nintendo's overall philosophy toward developing games, and how it extends to casual and competitive gamers. The Smash franchise's game designer Masahiro Sakurai himself expressed the concern that *"if we focus too much on the top-level players – or the audience – then the game skews a little bit too much on the technical side."* This is in-line with the company's overall approach to making games that appeal to casual players. With regard to professional gamers, Sakurai continued: *"It comes to a point where they're playing the game for the money, and I feel that kind of direction doesn't coincide with Nintendo's view of what games should be."* Nintendo

President Shuntaro Furukawa also echoed this view in an interview with Kyoto News earlier this year.

As Japan Esports Union's director Itsuki Murano commented following the release of the Switch: "*If the games makers themselves do not want to be involved in competitions, those games cannot be official esports games...It depends on Nintendo's brand strategies: is it a brand for playing at home or for competitions?*"

The Long Term Outlook is 'Peachy'

While Nintendo may currently consider itself a developer of solely casual games, the influence of players, company stakeholders, and Japan itself steer them toward greater involvement in esports over the coming years. The global esports audience is expected to reach 453.8 million this year and the esports industry is forecast to grow to $1.8 billion by 2022. Particularly given the popularity of Nintendo's platforms and some of their competitive titles, to forgo such a massive market opportunity could be heavily frowned upon by Nintendo's stakeholders. Moreover, with Japan beginning to allow domestically-held esports tournaments, the national shift in attitude may positively affect that of Nintendo. While Nintendo's support for competitive Splatoon 2 and Smash Ultimate may be limited for now to one-off, odd rule set tournaments held by the company, it is not hard to envisage the company taking a far more prominent and active role in the esports industry in the near future.

12

BLIZZARD'S CONTROVERSIAL 'BLITZCHUNG' RULING

The case of Chung 'Blitzchung' Ng Wai stands out of one of 2019's biggest stories due the incursion of sensitive political issues into esports and the breadth and severity of the backlash that it caused. Following Blizzard's initial ruling in October and our original report, the company reduced Ng Wai's lifetime ban to six months and returned his confiscated prize winnings. Blizzard President J. Allen Brack admitted at Blizzcon that the company "moved too quickly" in their ruling decision, but sentiment persists that Blitzchung deserves justice by commuting the rest of his ban before the start of the 2020 Hearthstone competitive season.

In early October, Blizzard crossed the line into world politics when it banned professional Hearthstone player Ng "Blitzchung" Wai Chung for making pro-Hong Kong protest remarks during a tournament stream. The incident follows a tough few days for the NBA which is weathering backlash over its handling of a tweet by Houston Rockets General Manager Daryl Morey's that also was supportive of the Hong Kong protest. While traditional sports and politics are no strangers, this is a relatively new development for esports, and the Blitzchung incident has sparked global outrage and raised questions across the esports industry, the wider video games community, and beyond, not only regarding the Hong Kong protests, but about freedom of speech, and China's involvement in and influence over overseas companies.

The Blitzchung Ruling

The initial incident took place during last Sunday's Asia-Pacific Hearthstone Grandmasters tournament. After winning the event, Chung was invited to a post-game interview on the official tournament stream. During the interview, Chung, originally from Hong Kong and an outspoken supporter of the ongoing protests against proposals to allow extradition to mainland China, donned a gas mask of the type worn by protestors, and exclaimed, *"Liberate Hong Kong. Revolution of our age!"* According to InvenGlobal, the two Taiwanese casters encouraged Chung to repeat the slogan in Mandarin for the audience to understand, and then cut the stream off.

Two days after the event, Blizzard issued a ruling that banned Chung from professional play for a year and revoked his tournament prize winnings. The company's reasoning was that Chung's actions violated Section 6.1 of the tournament rules:

"Engaging in any act that, in Blizzard's sole discretion, brings

you into public disrepute, offends a portion or group of the public, or otherwise damages Blizzard image will result in removal from Grandmasters and reduction of the player's prize total to $0 USD, in addition to other remedies which may be provided for under the Handbook and Blizzard's Website Terms."

Specifically, Chung's comments were deemed to have been "offensive" to the Chinese public. Blizzard also ceased working with the two casters that ran the stream that night, citing their cooperation with Chung.

Community Backlash

Blizzard's ruling was followed by immediate backlash across the global video gaming community. Forums and social media were flooded with comments in opposition, with many players stating that they would cancel their World of Warcraft accounts and uninstall other Blizzard titles. Activision Blizzard's stock price fell by 4% a result of the backlash. The popular Blizzard subreddit was closed for a time due to the volume and intensity of feedback on the topic. A popular Hearthstone caster Brian Kiebler announced that he will stop streaming and playing the game as a result of the company's decision. Even Senator Marco Rubio responded to the ruling, decrying China's influence on the global market and stating that, "*...implications of this will be felt long after everyone in U.S. politics today is gone.*"

Chinese Influence

As many of those in opposition to Activision Blizzard's ruling were quick to point, the company is partially owned by Chinese conglomerate Tencent. Tencent's stake in Blizzard is roughly 5% today, down from 15% prior to the Activision merger, but still a portion significant enough to be of influence. Moreover, the Chinese market is an increasingly important region for esports and Activision Blizzard. Blizzard's focus on the market is highlighted by their development of Diablo Immortal, which is created specifically for the Chinese mobile market. The World of Warcraft title was so popular in China that the subsequent movie release in the country made up for its disappointing US domestic return. To risk the ire of the Chinese government is, of course, to risk losing the regulatory approval required to operate in the potentially highly lucrative Chinese market. While Activision Blizzard is a predominantly Western-owned company, its reliance and degree to which it is influenced by the Chinese market are undeniable, and have been thrown into harsh light by the Blitzchung incident.

Legal Contexts of Free Speech

Blizzard's tournament rules have been crafted so as to provide broad legal coverage for issues such as the Chung ruling. The 2019 Hearthstone Grandmasters Official Competition Rules V1.4 states, *"Grandmasters players will be held to the highest standards of personal integrity and good sportsmanship."* As such, the company is free to determine its definition of "personal integrity" and what exactly *"brings you into public disrepute, offends a portion or group of the public, or otherwise damage's Blizzard image."*

Similar language providing for the protection of image can be found in Riot Games' official 2019 World Championship tournament rules, which state as follows:

"Team Members may not give, make, issue, authorize or endorse any statement or action having, or designed to have, an effect prejudicial or detrimental to the best interest of WCE, Riot Games or its affiliates, or League of Legends, as determined in the sole and absolute discretion of WCE."

This can be plainly interpreted that the company has the rights to determine what is acceptable speech. With Riot

Games being fully owned by Tencent, and Worlds now in full swing, it is not outside the realm of possibility that they may experience further incidents similar to and in reaction to the Blitzchung incident.

Whereas Blizzard and Riot's tournament rules assert a right to determine what types of speech will be allowed, Epic Games' recent statement about free speech provides interesting contrast. An Epic Games spokesperson told The Verge that, *"Epic supports everyone's right to express their views on politics and human rights. We wouldn't ban or punish a Fortnite player or content creator for speaking on these topics."*

This statement stands in spite of the fact that Tencent owns a 48.4% outstanding stake in the Fortnite publisher, which places Epic in the middle of the spectrum between Blizzard and Riot in terms of potential influence by Chinese shareholders. Epic Games taking this stance places them in opposition to two of the biggest esports companies in the world and the Chinese government. For how long Epic will maintain this stance is anybody's guess.

Will Companies or Community Set a Tone?

While politics have come to the forefront of discussion in esports before, such as regarding visa issues and what the vocational definition of an esports player should be, this is the first time for a political issue to reach such scope and scale in the industry. As esports continues to grow globally and reach new audiences, it is inevitable that further political lines will be crossed. Blizzard's ruling may set the current precedent for how sensitive PR situations are handled on the business side with Chinese stakeholders to appease, but as community fallout continues, we may see a change of tone in an effort to retain consumers in the Western market.

· · ·

UPDATE (10/12/19) Blizzard have issued an update regarding the Blitzchung incident, which you can read here: https://news.blizzard.com/en-us/blizzard/23185888/regarding-last-weekend-s-hearthstone-grandmasters-tournament

13

THE PRESENT STATE AND UNCERTAIN FUTURE OF ESPORTS PLAYERS' UNIONIZATION IN THE US

Given the existence of professional athlete unions in traditional sports in the US, the formation of an esports players' union would seem to be a natural development. However, while the will may be there, fragmentation, education, and motivation are at present forming barrier to progress. In a recent interview with WePlay!, Peter 'ppd' Dager of Ninjas in Pyjama's Dota 2 team stated that while many players would benefit from a union, wearing the hats of professional player and lobbyist for change would be difficult for those prefer to use their time to train for high-stakes events like The International.

Organization of professional esports players remains in its early stages, and a current characterization could be chaos and confusion. There has been much talk by current and former players about organizing, and this has intensified recently. A number of union organizations have in fact been established and launched. However, the funding and organizational resources supporting the largest and longest-established of these comes from game publishers rather than the players themselves. Since the publishers are often the very interests the players seek to gain leverage over by organizing in the first place, some have characterized these organizations as more akin to trade associations than labor unions. Some have even asked whether unionization is possible in the esports industry today, where fundamental questions such as whom players work for – and whether or not they are even in an employer-employee relationship – remain unclear.

All this notwithstanding, there is growing dissatisfaction among pro gamers over a range of issues, from the lack of transparency regarding how revenues are distributed to how, when and why publishers modify the video games being played. In view of the current situation, continued and increased organizing efforts by players to assert collective pressure to address their concerns would appear inevitable, but just where this might lead is still uncertain.

Game owners and league organizers are certainly aware of players' concerns and the potential damage that could be caused if their dissatisfaction is left unaddressed. In May 2016, esports organizer and production company Electronic Sports League (ESL) partnered with eight top esports teams to announce the formation of the World Esports Association (WESA) which, according to its press release at the time, "aims to bring much needed structure to a crowded esports ecosystem." Recognizing that players were an important part of the "ecosystem", WESA promised at the outset to provide the players with a seat at the table to "introduce elements of player representation" through a player-elected "Player Council". While WESA has succeeded in bringing some modest measure of organization to bear, it seems that the group has yet to deliver on the promises laid out the initial press release, although perhaps to expect this within three years would be unrealistic.

In June 2017, concurrent with Riot Games' announcement of its franchise system for the North American *League of Legends* Championship Series, the company announced that the league would have an official players association which, it emphasized, would have full autonomy. Shortly after the formation of the association, Hal Biagas, former assistant general counsel at the National Basketball Players Association, was appointed head of the organization. Riot Games has perhaps moved *League of Legends* pro players a step closer to unionization, but this is still not a players' union, nor could it be under US federal law so long as it is funded by Riot Games.

In 2018 esports media was abuzz with news that the formation of two esports players' organizations was under discussion. It was reported that approximately seventy *CS:GO* professional gamers had signed membership letters signaling their intent to become members of the Counter-Strike Professional Players Association (CSPPA). The CSPPA was established by former player and esports broadcaster Scott 'SirScoots' Smith. The organization's website states that it offers collective representation in ongoing dialogues with industry stakeholders and contract negotiation services to any player who is contracted or is actively seeking a contract as a professional Counter Strike player at an "elite" level. The organization is still in its infancy and it is difficult to predict what it may be able to accomplish for players. The CSPPA, however, is not a labor union. In fact, the organization emphasizes that the "membership letters" players sign are not union authorization cards, which would be needed to organize as a labor union under the National Labor Relations Act and the rules of the National Labor Relations Board. In addition, the CSPPA is organized internationally, which presents another hurdle to US unionization.

Around the same time that the CSPPA was announced, former *Overwatch* player and coach Thomas "Morte" Kerbusch announced plans to organize an *Overwatch* players association. There has been little visible, public activity related to the organization since the announcement was made.

Observers who are quick to draw conclusions about the future of player unionization in esports based upon the developments (or lack thereof) in the past decade should consider the historical development of unionization in traditional sports. Eighty-one years passed from the formation of the Brotherhood of Professional Baseball Players in 1885 to the recognition of the Major League Baseball Players Association by team owners in 1966. Fifty years of fits, starts and turmoil preceded the certification in 1960 by the National Labor Relations Board of the NFL players union. The NBA took over a decade to move from early organizing efforts to union recognition in 1964.

In each of these cases there was a single league of players playing the same sport. The teams, their owners and the players were all within the United States. It was clear in each case who owned the teams and who employed the players. By contrast, in esports there are multiple leagues organized by many different organizers, not all of whom have the same interests in the industry. There are dozens of different games being played in these leagues by players who are playing in countries all over the globe.

All the legal and practical difficulties associated with

organizing esports players' unions aside, the pressure to organize collectively will remain and only continue to grow as the esports industry continues to mature. At this time, how this pressure will manifest itself, be it in the formation of a union or unions in the traditional legal sense or not, is still far from clear.

14

JAPAN'S '1ST ESPORTS EVENT FOR DISABLED' HIGHLIGHTS INCLUSIVITY IN ESPORTS AND POSITIVE SOCIAL CHANGE

The announcement of Japan's '1st eSports Event for Disabled" was widely lauded by English-language media, but the actual event was far less widely covered. Fortunately, notice was taken in Japan; since the publication of our article, Japanese football club Nagoya Grampus has begun to work with local companies to provide an esports practice space and organize tournaments for differently-abled esports players in a move that brings together traditional sports and esports, and helps to further dismantle the stereotypes and obstacles surrounding disabled individuals in the country.

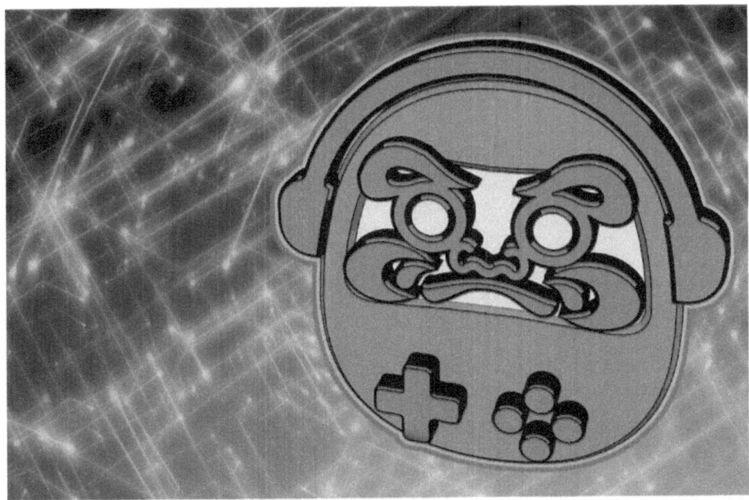

In August 2019, Gunma eSports Association in Japan held the world's first-ever disabled esports event, '1st eSports Event for Disabled in 2019 GUNMA'. Japan's initiation and hosting of this event highlights positive and significant shifts in attitudes towards the disabled in Japan that have occurred in recent years and are paving the path toward the 2020 Tokyo Olympics and Paralympics.

From the late 19th century, Japanese political and scientific thought were influenced by Western-based beliefs and practices concerning eugenics. Legal acts such as the National Eugenic Law of 1940 and the Eugenic Protection Law of 1948 were passed with the objective of removing "negative" physical and mental attributes from the Japanese populace. These acts permitted forced sterilization in cases where prefectural government deemed an individual to possess a serious genetic disorder. The eugenics law was finally abolished in 1996 with the Mother's Body Protection Law. A joint bill recently passed to compensate Japanese citizens who were affected by the now-banned practices.

Gunma eSports Association logo

· · ·

With the Gunma event, esports is now playing a part in driving such progress. Esports is rapidly gaining traction in Japan, creating a new platform for thought, discussion, and action on a variety of social and economic issues. While video games are a long-established industry in the home country of Sony and Nintendo, and Japan is currently the third largest gaming market in the world, Japanese esports only took off from early 2018, following the establishment of the Japanese eSports Union. Since this time, esports in Japan has experienced explosive growth and engendered changes in social consciousness and dialogue; in fact, 'esports' was voted as a national buzzword in 2018. Arguably one of the defining characteristics of esports is inclusivity: esports titles inherently involve competing or cooperating with others, gender need not be so rigorously divided as is the case in traditional sports, and it is not the sole purview of physically gifted individuals. This inclusivity also extends to those who have physical disabilities, so it makes sense for esports to stand as a platform for representation of the disabled.

Indeed, there are already several organizations that exist to promote the representation of disabled people in esports. AbleGamers Foundation and Charity is a public charity in the United States that has supported events for gamers with disabilities since 2004. This organization has opened up 'accessibility arcades' in several cities, and assists disabled players to acquiring specialized adaptable hardware. One AbleGamers affiliate, Dayton 'Wheels' Jones, commented on the impact: *"I love watching sports and talking about it, but I can't partake in it. Gaming is something you can win in, improve in, gain rewards from, and be known as a champion in and I love doing it."*

The Japanese organization OneLife, Inc. has recently undertaken to create exactly this type of facility in Japan.

OneLife has quietly taken the AbleGamers approach to accessibility arcades and created specialized training centers for disabled gamers, which allows players to utilize practice rooms like the ones normally only available to non-disabled players. OneLife also produces equipment to facilitate gaming for gamers of different ability levels. These are meaningful resources, especially for those who wish to play esports titles that are highly dependent on peripheral ergonomics and dexterity.

OneLife's efforts eventually led to '1st eSports Event for Disabled in 2019 GUNMA', which was held at Big Cube in Gunma, and acted as a vehicle to promote the activities of the organization. Organizers centered the event around a 1,000,000 JPY prize for a major League of Legends tournament, which was supported in part by Unsold Stuff Gaming, a major pro esports team in Japan. Anyone with a disability certificate was eligible for entry. Sports marketing agency Roxstate also sponsored the event, as featured on the company website. The event put on immersive displays of accessible gaming equipment, promoted empathic feedback from observers, and celebrated when a team called 'Wallbreakers' won the League of Legends win, as reported by Japanese gaming site GAME Watch. The team's leader, GreenBird, who is diagnosed on the autism spectrum, celebrated the win on his personal Twitter account.

The fact that this event gained wide coverage both domestically and internationally not only showed esports as a positive and forward-thinking industry, but brought light to Japan's significant social and legislative progress with regards to disabled people. As more outlets recognize OneLife and Gunma eSports' contributions to the dialogue about disability, it is very likely that societal perceptions and attitudes will continue change for the better, not only for gamers, but for Japan as a whole. This increased awareness, coupled with the

International Paralympics Committee's newly released video game, "The Pegasus Dream Tour," will usher in 2020 with more positivity towards differently-abled individuals.

15

WHY ISN'T RUSSIA AN ESPORTS SUPERPOWER?

S ince the publication of this article, Russia is still making strides to catch up with other countries and boosting its profile in the esports industry. One recent step is the announcement of the EPICENTER 2020 Dota 2 Major tournament. Scheduled to take place in May 2020 in Moscow, this $1 million dollar prize pool event will draw eyes to the best teams in the region and will serve as one of the last stops towards the International 10. It is clout-raising events like this that will help Russia on its way to potentially achieving esports superpower status.

. . .

When the Russian government officially recognized esports as a national sport in 2001, it set a precedent for the rest of the world. As the first country to acknowledge esports on this level, Russia seemed to be staking an early position as an industry leader. However despite this initiative and an active player base, years of false starts and economic and political turbulence have set the country back from achieving its esports potential. As of 2018, Russia was ranked only eleventh in the global gaming market by number of players and amounts spent.

Early Competitive Gaming in Russia

The fall of the Soviet Union and the rise of internet access in the 1990s transformed Russia rapidly from a relatively closed nation. As most homes did not have a personal computer or access to web services, internet cafes thrived in this period. It was at these cafes that Russian youths first got their hands on popular PC games, in most cases through pirated versions. PCs were the go-to gaming device due to the scarcity and cost of console hardware and software in the Russian market.

Quake, Counter-Strike, Age of Empires, Unreal Tournament and StarCraft were the principal early esports games played into the early 2000s in Russian internet cafes and home PCs once they began to proliferate. This growth was timely, as global interest in "cyber games" resulted in the formation of organizations such as the Electronic Sports League and World Cyber Games. In response, the Russian Esports Federation (ReSF) was founded in 2000 with the objective of organizing events and advocating for esports recognition in the country. Russians then began to compete in some of the new international tournaments, which in turn raised the profile of esports at home. When Russia declared esports a national sport in 2001, it was the first country in the world to do so.

False Starts

With esports officially recognized, Russia had the opportunity to be a world leader in the industry. However, this potential was not to be realized and growth of esports in Russia was significantly less than the leading esports countries. For example, the Korean eSports Association was founded the same year as the ReSF, yet was able to quickly mobilize to execute and broadcast esports games. This led to the professionalization of esports in South Korea and that country becoming the most advanced esports country, even without the state-level of recognition that esports had in Russia. Moreover, a few years later and following an administration change in 2006, the status of esports as a national sport in Russia was revoked.

The false start of esports as a national initiative in Russia has been attributed to a lack of funding and the country's complex bureaucracy. In 2005, the RAND Corporation reported that, *"Major personnel changes and organizational realignments that Putin unveiled in March 2004, while simplifying the government structure at the top, created widespread uncertainty and upset long-term planning below, including planning for IT investments."* This would have affected the esports sector, which was dependent on the same IT and internet funding.

In addition to changes in government in the mid-2000s, Russia was embroiled in international disputes relating to Georgia and Ukraine. This period coincidentally aligned with what Complexity Gaming's Founder Jason Lake called the global esports scene's *"dark times of near obscurity circa 2007-8,"* otherwise known as the 'esports bust period'. It would be years before Russia even considered reinstating any form of competitive video gaming on the national sports register.

Survival and Resurgence

While esports was certainly down at this point, it was far from out and soon experienced growth again. Russian players continued to compete in domestic tournaments and larger events were held in Moscow. The World Cyber Games consistently held annual Russian national events in the capital, which was and still is the epicenter for esports activity in the country. Other events such as the Global Amusement Moscow Exhibition (GameX) in 2007, organized for international competition with a dollar prize pool equivalent of 1,500,000 rubles (approximately $60,000 at the time), kept esports alive in Russia. By the late 2000s, many skilled teams and individuals were making a mark on the scene by winning prizes in games such as Warcraft II, StarCraft, and Counter-Strike.

With the release of StarCraft II in 2010 and the popularization of streaming platforms like Justin.tv (later to become Twitch), esports in Russian continued to grow in scale. Moscow continued to be a popular esports event location, and games such as Counter-Strike: Global Offensive and Dota 2 drew increasing numbers of players on their releases in 2012 and 2013 respectively. World of Tanks was able to amass a player base of up to 37 million players, showcasing the potential of Eastern Europe as a developer as well as a consumer of esports titles.

Due to this measured growth and developing success, Russia reinstated esports as an officially recognized sport in 2016. Thanks to the economic success of the 2010s and a core spot on the Russian Sport Register, Russian investors finally began to support esports in earnest.

. . .

Recent Investments and Future Potential

Epicenter, a series of events held in Moscow and St. Petersburg and run by the Russian esports organizer ESForce provides one example of the results of investment in esports in Russia. Esports has also found favor among Russian financial heavyweights. In 2018 Casino News Daily reported that ESForce was acquired for $100 million by Mail.ru, owned by Russian magnate Alisher Usmanov. It also reported that private investor Nikolai Belykh purchased a 25% stake in the pro team and computer club Winstrike for $10 million.

While the recent growth and support have been helped to raise the status of esports in Russia, there are other issues that Russia must overcome before it can be considered to be on the road to becoming an esports superpower. The country's players often run into visa issues when attempting to compete internationally. While some of these visa issues are domestic in nature, others are international, as has been the case for tournaments in Germany, the United States and Ukraine. In 2014, the "Moscow Five" were unable to compete at IEM Cologne for League of Legends due to unspecified "visa issues". They went on to state in official social media posts that they will need to be more "scrupulous" in future when applying for European Union entry. In 2017, Denis "Tonic" Rulev was denied entry to the US to play in an Overwatch contenders tournament. More recently Gambit Esports were almost denied entry in Ukraine to play in the Starladder Dota 2 tournament.

While Russia may have some challenges to overcome before it attains a leading position in global esports, it is on the way to becoming the third-largest gaming market in Europe according to a recent Supercell/Wargaming digital gaming report. The continued growth in the video games and esports industries combined with increasing investment and the increasingly higher profile of esports on a global level may provide the fuel that Russia needs to achieve esports superpower status in future.

VIRTUAL AND
AUGMENTED REALITY

16

VR AND MENTAL HEALTH

The impact of VR on mental health will become more apparent as increasing numbers of people buy and use VR devices that offer increasingly immersive experiences. At present, VR is both a potential catalyst for addiction, escapism, isolation, and other mentally-unhealthy actions and a useful and beneficial tool in the mental health industry. One positive use case, VRET (virtual reality exposure therapy), is used to help people overcome post-traumatic stress disorder by offering a safe place to confront imagery that patients find disturbing. The same is true for the treatment of phobias and anxiety. As of now, whether VR ultimately serves to benefit mental health more than it negatively impacts it still remains to be seen.

In drama, there's this fascinating convention called The Fourth Wall. The Fourth Wall is the term used to describe the way in which the actors in a live theatrical performance pretend there's an invisible wall between themselves and the audience. The audience can see through the pretend wall, and watch the players, but the players pretend the wall is real, and have to act as if they're unaware they're being watched. It's a remarkable bit of artifice, because, of course, being watched is the entire point of the exercise. In certain modern forms of drama, the wall is eliminated, and the players will come out and directly address the audience, but that's more the exception than the rule.

The wall exists in films and television, too, thanks to the limits of technology. You are watching the action, from the other side of a screen, and you can always look away, stop the film, or whatever. There is still and always the option of not participating in the process. In the end, the audience members have the option of observing or not.

This is a way of preserving the integrity of the narrative. The equivalent of the way a book works – word by word, page by page, chapter by chapter – is a movie, play or television show in which the people who are watching collectively agree not to interfere in the process, and let the play take them where it will. It's not immersive, because immersion would mean participation, which would disrupt the story-telling.

The entire point of virtual reality is, of course, precisely this immersion. In VR, the audience and the event are one thing. The wall is gone. You're not watching something unfold, you're part of it. This gives VR an overwhelming degree of immediacy and impact. It's one thing to watch the action from the fixed location of your seat, as it occurs behind a conceptual wall. It's quite another to be standing in the middle of it, moving through it and effectively part of it. For an adult, passing through the wall is a very powerful experience. Scientists, however, are now beginning to explore whether for children, and perhaps for some susceptible adults, the experience could actually be damaging. Given the popularity and growth of VR, the legal liability this would produce is enormous. Viewed from 30,000 feet, the subject of unexpected forms of liability and damages arising from VR use is a case study in how legal theories coalesce around a new technology, and how adoption and disruption have the potential for unintended legal consequences.

When it comes to VR, there are two general categories of this kind of potential injury. The first is vision. In the real world, your eyes focus and converge on the same point in space. If you're looking at a tree on the other side of a meadow, your eyes automatically focus for that distance, and look at it. These two mechanisms work together, in an automatic function called the accommodation-convergence reflex.

VR is different. It basically works by fooling your eyes. The actual object you're focusing on is exactly the same distance away all the time – the VR screen. However, on the screen, images represent objects that may look near or may look far away, and so the automatic reflex is replaced by an artificially created conflict. This can occasionally be disorienting, but the effect is short-lived. Typically, the effects of this, as with most of the other effects of VR, rapidly disappear when the headset's removed. Your brain, and eye, adjust back to the real world from the virtual world and it's all good.

A similar effect occurs when you're looking at a VR display on a stereoscopic screen. The real world, of course, isn't divided into two separate visual experiences which your brain unifies. However, VR headsets working by fooling your brain into seeing one thing, even though you're exposed to two displays. In both cases, the eyes need to adjust to an unnatural environment, and with the exception of a few isolated examples, adjust back after a few seconds of looking at the real world. At least so far, adults have no problem with VR.

The potential problem – and legal liabilities – may arise when children begin using VR systems, particularly in large numbers and for extended periods of time. The current behavior of young people with smartphones is a testament to the way kids can become absorbed in a technology, literally to the exclusion of everything else. If you've ever seen a group of kids together, and all simultaneously staring at their phones, you know what I mean. There's no reason to think that VR will be any exception to this trend. And while no conclusive evidence of any form of visual impairment has yet been observed, the projected enormous growth of the use and ubiquity of VR, particularly among young people who brains and therefore visual systems are still developing presents what can be described an as-yet-unknown hazard. If it emerges, the impact will be enormous. Millions of children with visual problems exacerbated by VR is a class-action attorney's dream. Given the plaintiff bar's aggressiveness and skill at coming up with new theories of liability, it's simply a matter of time until the allegations of damage caused by prolonged VR use have some kind of a day in court.

The second potential category of VR problems like this are, of all things, mental. The immersive, overwhelming experience of VR may, it seems, present a mental health hazard to people who are already struggling with, or vulnerable to, various mental or emotional maladies.

There are already documented, isolated examples of people allegedly suffering from addiction to video games. In one widely-shared example, a young Chinese gamer allegedly died after spending nineteen consecutive hours playing World of Warcraft. The examples of death or injury claimed to be from video game addiction are rare, and to this point, anecdotal.

However, mental health professionals have already

expressed some concern about the potential for significant challenges virtual reality presents to people who are already afflicted with mental or emotional disorders. VR, of course, is an enormously affecting experience, with an environment that literally supplants reality. Remember the missing Fourth Wall. In addition, because it is so immersive, it also is a vastly more stimulating experience. It's much more arousing to the brain and neuroendocrine systems, which is a recipe for abuse and addiction. Pharmaceuticals do exactly the same thing, simply using chemicals in place of visual and auditory effects.

The therapeutic potential of VR for people grappling with emotional, behavioral or mental challenges is substantial. But by the same token, it's also easy to visualize VR as a kind of self-medication. If interacting with the real world is challenging or traumatic, imagine the allure of substituting an elaborate virtual alternative. Many mental disorders include issues with discerning between fantasy and reality, and take forms as diverse as paranoia, delusions, adjustment disorders, and in the most severe examples, outright psychosis, including hallucinations.

If the line between fantasy and reality simply failed to exist at all, as might be the case with VR abuse, then rather than helping treat and resolve mental disorders, VR was used to exacerbate them, the liabilities would be enormous, particularly those arising from harm or danger occasioned by VR-powered delusions or other behavior. This would be especially true if abuse of virtual reality was also combined with some sort of drug dependency.

Similarly, this same form of self-medication use of VR could simply delay treatment or make it pointless. A wife and mother who suffers from depression, and finds it appealing to spend days inside a nonexistent virtual world rather than wrestling her emotional demons to the ground in therapy arguably had VR make her symptoms made worse. The legal implications of this are enormous. The very potency of the virtual experience also presents very real risks of abuse, addiction and possibly damage of the most profound sort.

And as always, the technology is new, the potential is enormous, the growth is rapid, and the conclusion again (and perhaps somewhat ironically) remains: wait and see.

17

VR, AR AND LOADING A C-5

ITAR compliance continues to be a confusing burden for many new tech startups that are unused to such stringent regulation as well as established tech companies that are making forays into emerging technologies. Even Microsoft's Holo-Lens has been subject to review for compliance with ITAR regulations, for export classification and also for its potential as a prototyping platform for objects that could then easily be 3D printed.

Similarly, the use of SaaS and cloud servers for data storage in VR and AR applications raise security concerns, as companies that would be subject to ITAR compliance must ensure that all servers and transmissions occur on US soil until certification status is established.

One of the earliest, and most consistent users of virtual reality has been the military. In all kinds of military jobs, VR provides a way to enhance work to make it more accurate, more efficient, and less prone to costly mistakes. One example is the work of a "loadmaster", the person responsible for loading, unloading and properly balancing the cargo inside a military transport. By augmenting what a loadmaster sees inside the cargo space of a plane, the vital, error-intolerant work of properly arranging and securing the tons of material inside a cargo plane can be accelerated, and made much more reliable.

VR is widely used in the military for similar situations, in which routine tasks or dynamic environments have to be mastered with zero margin for error. Examples include flight simulation for pilots and crews, battlefield simulation for ground troops, medic training for corpsmen and other battlefield personnel, weapons practice and training and as with the loadmaster software, vehicle simulation. Also, given that a lot of what the military actually does costs large amounts of money, or is extremely dangerous, military operations are a perfect environment for AR.

Loading a military cargo plane is complex, high-stakes work. It often has to be done under a lot of stress, or in difficult environments. Errors can down the plane. So, AR is an excellent way to augment what the loadmaster actually sees and does during preflight checks, to make sure there are no mistakes and nothing's missed. Interestingly, though, the use of AR/VR for military purposes can become a national security matter, which makes some software subject to an entirely new regulatory scheme – export controls. Augmented reality systems to aid in loading cargo planes, according to the relevant authorities, is a military asset. It's considered a "munition". Which is a whole other area of law that the VR/AR industry is increasingly having to come to grips with.

In 1976, the U.S. government enacted ITAR, an acronym

for International Traffic in Arms Regulations. Originally put in place during the end of the Cold War, this set of regulations was (and is) intended to safeguard United States national security and further US foreign interests by regulating the import or export of defense-related items, which include both physical objects and professional services. The simple, obvious idea was to control which countries had access to which US military assets, to insure that we weren't, in effect, arming those perceived as enemies of the US. Increasingly, military assets also include technology, particularly defense-related software and now, virtual and augmented reality. The system for loadmasters is an example.

When it was originally developed, ITAR was focused on the classic, typical tools of warfare – ships. Aircraft. Naval vessels. Tangible objects that actually did things. Technology was in its infancy. The last Apollo moon mission ended just four years before ITAR was enacted, and it's helpful to remember that the computing power for those missions was incredibly primitive – a smartphone is millions of times faster and more powerful than the computers used to send men to the moon.

However, as the definition of warfare, and the role of technology in it, rapidly broadened, the definition of "munition" had to grow as well to include software, satellites, everything that went into modern war fighting. For example, GPS satellites, which now power everything from the direction system in rental cars to cruise missiles, wasn't even begun until 1978, but now, satellites and related technology are a fundamental, and closely monitored, category of military assets under ITAR. The loadmaster AR system, made by a company called Navmar, is another.

Founded in 1977, Navmar Applied Sciences is one of thousands of small and medium-sized defense contractors around the country. Headquartered in a suburb of Philadelphia, Navmar began by developing and marketing "highly specialized acoustics engineering and analysis support to the Naval Air Warfare Center in Warminster, Pennsylvania. Here our engineering staff worked in concert with naval base researchers to develop new innovations in anti-submarine warfare." In the past forty years, the company has grown to over 200 employees, at ten locations around the country. They now provide dozens of products and services in in six different categories, one of which is the loadmaster augmented reality platform. Which is governed by ITAR.

For companies in the virtual reality business, this creates a new kind of regulatory obligation that conceivably applies to almost everyone. In addition to the typical legal issues any business faces, VR/AR companies also have to grapple with the process of having their technology reviewed, and a determination made as to where and how it fits into the regulatory scheme of ITAR. Conventional defense contractors are used to this – they've been doing it for a long time. But for tech companies, especially fast-growing, early-stage VR companies, this is something new, and something really, really important.

There are a number of different potential outcomes in the ITAR certification process for a company's software, which are far too complex to describe in a blog post. Suffice to say that it's a specialty unto itself. The ideal outcome is a declaration that a company's product is an "EAR99", meaning, overall, it's not classified as a military-related product, and typically doesn't require an export license. This isn't completely the end of the story – you still need to insure that the product isn't being diverted to a prohibited country, or used for a prohibited purpose, for example. But an EAR99 classification is a very desirable thing.

But the main point here is that having this determination made is not optional. Penalties for noncompliance, and/or not obtaining a license are severe, and include both fines and jail time. "Severe" means a fine of a million dollars per violation, applicable retroactively The best advice is this – if you're involved in virtual or augmented reality at all, it's a very good idea to find out whether and how your product or service fits into the enormous machinery of ITAR, and above all, not to overlook it. This is about national defense, homeland security and an entire ecosystem of regulatory actors who you neglect at your peril.

18

QUALITY OF USER EXPERIENCE IS DRIVING VR/AR SALES

By Q3 2019, screenless VR viewers were down to 13.2% unit share, according to IDC — a slightly lower drop than expected. Users continue to favor toward standalone and tethered units for experience quality and entertainment value. Retailers took advantage of this trend during 2019's Black Friday and Cyber Monday by offering major discounts on these types of units. Target discounted a PlayStation VR bundle by $100, Game-Stop offered the HTC Vive Pro Starter Kit for $300 below MSRP, and Wal-Mart discounted the Oculus Go by $50 over the sale period. The discounts were well received and many locations sold out.

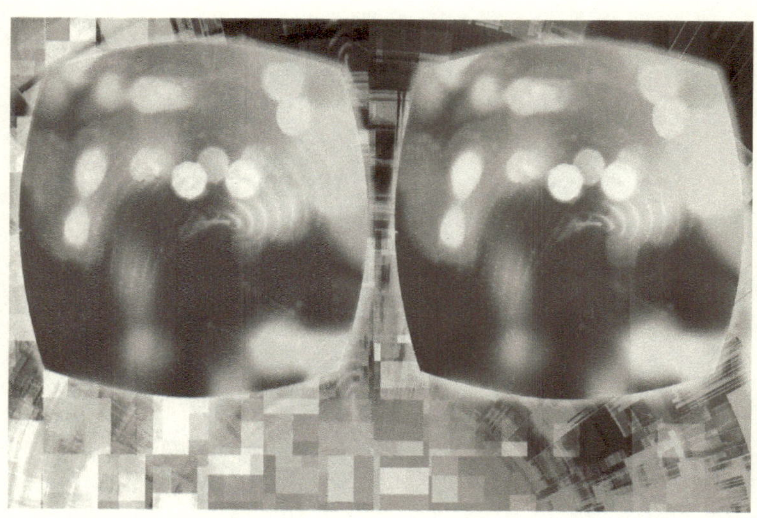

Recent sales figures and forecasts indicate that high-quality user experience is a principal factor driving VR/AR hardware sales, a fact that bodes well for the market.

The Novelty is Wearing off... for the Better

IDC predicts that the VR/AR market will grow at a compound annual growth rate of 66.7% from 2019 to 2023, with unit sales expected to reach 68.6 million units. Segmented sales data shows that the VR/AR market is now moving towards platforms that prioritize quality of experience over other factors. Standalone headsets are expected to have the fastest growth rates, followed by tethered headsets. However, lower-cost screenless viewers such as Google Cardboard or Samsung Gear VR have slowed considerably.

This trend suggests that consumers are moving on from VR as a novelty and starting to embrace VR as a serious entertainment experience. In the short term, this is causing product rotation as customers purchase more expensive headsets. For example, in 2018 screenless viewers made up 29% of units sold, and this category is expected to drop to 15% in 2019.

Quality First

In 2018, Sony (PlayStation VR), Facebook (Oculus), and HTC accounted for 77% of headset revenue. These vendors provide the flagship headsets for quality of user experience at competitive prices. Vendors that have focused on factors such as reducing cost and ease of setup at the expense of user experience have been losing market share.

Vendors of integrated headsets are arguably better positioned to incorporate technological advancements moving forward, as advancements in 5G, sensor intelligence, and cloud-based computing have the potential to reduce size and weight, improve the form factors of VR/AR hardware, and increase the all-important 'cool' factor while improving ease of setup and use.

VR Sales Momentum is Strong

In March this year, Sony announced it had sold 4.2 million units of the PlayStation VR. Then during an analyst meeting in July, Mark Zuckerberg, the CEO of Facebook, suggested Oculus headsets were also selling well, stating, *"This quarter, we shipped Oculus Quest, our first all-in-one headset with no wires and full freedom of movement. It has gotten great reviews and we're selling them as fast as we can make them. More importantly, we've delivered an experience that people keep using week after week, and buying more content."* Some analysts are predicting that the Quest will sell over 1.3 million units in 2019.

In June, Steam saw an 80% year-on-year increase in connected headsets. Steam also had over 1 million connected users during the month of June. It is predicted that based on current user growth rates, Steam will have over 2 million VR users per month by 2020.

Location, Location, Location

The user adoption rate for location-based VR (LBVR) is similarly positive, demonstrating that customers are willing to pay for high quality out-of-home VR experiences. For example, Munich-based startup Hologate is experiencing a steady increase of about 200,000 players per month. Hologate is currently active in 21 countries and 250 locations. The average Hologate operator serves1,500 players per month.

Los Angeles-based Tyffon Inc. has been raising capital to expand its location footprint. Tyffon's investors include Tokyo Broadcasting Systems, Sega Sammy Holdings, The Walt

Disney Company, Mizuho Capital, Tokyu Recreation and Canal Ventures. Tyffon will open a third Tokyo location this year. Currently the company has locations in the Odaiba and Shibuya districts of Tokyo and will open a "Tyffonium" in Los Angeles this year.

SpringboardVR, which offers an LBVR platform for location operators, expects to be supporting 1,000 locations by the end of the year.

The scale and scope of LBVR partnerships and licensing agreements are on the increase. For example, ILMxLAB and The Void collaborated to produce a free-roam Star Wars VR experience in Star Wars: Secrets of the Empire, which released in January this year. The title has been well-received, potentially paving the way for future movie franchise and VR collaborations.

According to Cliff Plumer, CEO of The Void, "*As the first project to collaborate with the Walt Disney Company on one of the biggest IPs in the world, it was thrilling and frightening all at the same time. We knew going into it that the quality of work and the bar would be raised high. We had no choice but to achieve what Walt Disney Studio and Star Wars fans expected.*"

The below table presents the current number of locations for major LBVR players, though many plan to continue expanding and open new locations in the short term.

Name	# of Locations	Capital Raised (USD Millions)	URL
Hologate	250	NA	http://hologate.com
Zero Latency	32	8.9	https://zerolatencyvr.com
The Void	29	20	https://thevoid.com
Sandbox VR	12	71	https://sandboxvr.com
Tyffon	4	12	https://www.tyffon.com
Dreamscape	2	36.7	https://dreamscapeimmersive.com
Nomadic	2	6	https://blurtheline.com

The Outlook for Now is Positive

While VR/AR has receded from the headlines following the boom of recent years, recent sales data and forecasts are positive, and trends point to increasing sophistication of both supply and demand in the market, facts that bode well for the long term outlook of this very much still-developing sector.

19

ELEVEN CRIMES THAT OCCUR
IN VIRTUAL REALITY

As a side note, virtual reality is being used to re-enact real crimes by analysts and other law enforcement professionals. In one instance, convicted burglars recreate their crimes in VR, offering deep insight to analysts about the methods and thought processes of these criminals. This data can then be used in tandem with artificial intelligence to predict which locations are at the highest risk of becoming criminal hotspots. Similarly, VR is being used in courtrooms to examine crime scenes from a variety of angles—even allowing observers to pick up objects—without disturbing real-world evidence.

. . .

While still in the early stages of adoption, virtual reality already plays host to a range of criminal activities, from extortion and terrorism to money laundering and prostitution. The law has yet to fully catch up with crimes in virtual reality, but the types of harm that can be done in virtual worlds and their implications are becoming increasingly better understood as the technology grows in popularity.

In 2019, in the US alone, 42.9 million people will use virtual reality. Virtual worlds are increasing in number, popularity, and complexity, and giving rise to interesting legal questions and problems. Some forms of criminal activity map over directly from the real world, but even these can raise legal questions, for example regarding jurisdiction. In the civil context, if two parties sign a contract in a virtual world, which state's or country's laws should govern the contract if not specified in the contract itself?

Depending on the situation, the distinction between what constitutes actual crime and what is simply 'virtual' crime is unclear; such situations are causing lawyers, psychologists, sociologists, and other experts to reconsider what is actually damaging and what should be considered criminal. For example, if someone were to "physically" assault another person in VR, so causing them to experience distress or even a physical sensation of pain, should that be treated in the same way as physical harm in the real world? Given the relative immaturity of the virtual reality industry, many of these questions are presently unanswered.

Death Threats and Assault

Since many virtual reality games involve "killing" other players, death threats are a common occurrence in these settings. The differentiating factor between 'smack talk' or role-play and true, criminal death threats is intent. In VR, a death threat that is an actual display of aggression and intent can be a visceral experience, particularly if you can see the virtual representation of the threatening individual. While the laws vary by US state, any form of expression of harm with the intent to scare or actually harm another can be considered assault.

Money Laundering

Money laundering is "the process of disguising the proceeds of crime and integrating it into the legitimate financial system." Many virtual worlds have their own currency system which users can purchase with fiat currency and then use to buy digital items and services within the virtual world. In countries where financial regulation is outpaced by technology, this can create a safe haven for criminal activity including money laundering. In such cases, criminals simply exchange illegally obtained money for in-game currency.

Terrorism

Terrorism has already infiltrated the virtual world. Not only are counterterrorism officers training on virtual terrorists, but terrorists are able to use virtual reality to plan, strategize, simulate, and train for terrorist attacks. Perhaps even more problematically, these platforms can also be used for recruitment purposes as terrorist propaganda can be presented in more visceral and compelling ways than other media and platforms. Virtual reality can be used by terrorist organizations to train recruits on the use of weaponry as well as to desensitize them to scenarios that may result from their actions. These techniques are also employed by the US military.

. . .

Intellectual Property Theft

The theft of intellectual property is a longtime and pervasive issue in both analog and digital worlds, and this carries over into virtual reality. For example, virtual reality content creators may produce virtual clothing that includes trademarked brand names for their avatars to wear or even use celebrity likenesses as those avatars. While some cases are clear cut infringements of intellectual property rights, questions such as what constitutes fair use in the virtual world cause complications and gray areas.

Child Abuse Media

The exchange of digital media that portrays the abuse of real children is an ongoing crime in the digital world which also follows into virtual reality. The exchange of imagery portraying real world people and situations is definitively a crime, whether in the virtual world or not. However, the line becomes blurred as it pertains to age play in the virtual world. While the US has ruled that a consenting adult portraying themselves (by a virtual avatar) as a child and engaging in explicit acts falls within the realm of fantasy and are not criminal. This does not extend to other countries, however, and does not account for increasingly real depictions as VR fidelity becomes more sophisticated.

Fraud and Cybercrime

Cybercrime is an issue almost anywhere there is an internet connection (and sometimes even when there isn't). Taking advantage of the opportunities presented by virtual reality simply represents an extension of the real-world activities of criminals who defraud people and systems in other digital environments such as within online games.

· · ·

Stalking and Griefing

Cyberstalking is a crime wherein criminals use digital means to invade privacy and harass others, usually with obsessive fervor. This behavior can carry into virtual reality, although the experience may become even more disconcerting for the victim due to the immersive nature of the technology. People, sometimes in groups, who do this for the sake of intimidation and harassment, are often referred to as "griefers."

Prostitution

Virtual reality can be used as a setting in which to arrange real-world sexual encounters for money, but prostitution within virtual worlds can also be a criminal act subject to prosecution. In some jurisdictions, paying for even simulated sexual contact, such as that between avatars, may be considered prostitution and is punishable by law.

Sexual Assault

Because of the immersive nature of virtual reality, victims of sexual assault in virtual reality can experience many of the same feelings and issues as victims who have been subject to the crime in the physical world. However, some of the consequences of sexual assault in virtual reality obviously differ from the possible real-world physical consequences, and as a result, the degree of severity which with it is treated can vary, and as in the real world, the definition of what does and does not constitute sexual assault can vary widely depending upon the situation and jurisdiction.

· · ·

Extortion

The Chinese government imprisoned a known gang member for three years for extorting virtual goods and currency. As we spend more of our time in our increasingly real and complex virtual worlds, the items within them will grow in value to us. This will make virtual reality ripe for criminals who care to use extortion.

Identity Theft

There are two sides of identity theft in virtual reality, one of which is illegal and another which frequently is legally ambiguous. The first case is identity theft in the traditional sense, in which a criminal uses a virtual reality platform to represent themselves as another person, perhaps to utilize their credit to buy costly goods or perhaps for more nefarious purposes.

The second case involves theft or misappropriation of a virtual identity. In many forms of virtual reality, users utilize an avatar which is linked to their own identity and is the equivalent of their physical body in the real world. What if other players "steal" their likeness? What if they pose as another user in order to defame them? What if they hold this identity as a form of blackmail? Virtual reality and identity together pose a lot of questions, so naturally, the idea of identity theft in virtual reality does too.

20

CAN "VR SICKNESS" PROVIDE THE BASIS FOR A SUCCESSFUL CLASS ACTION OR PERSONAL INJURY LAWSUIT?

Major VR equipment manufacturers currently recommend that users take a 10–15 minute break every half hour regardless of whether or not they feel that they need it, because extended VR usage can result in many of the symptoms of VR sickness. While there is a variety of methods claimed to reduce VR sickness, such as using Dramamine, eating ginger, or wearing a wristband, the prevalence and seriousness of this phenomenon may still give cause for some users to seek legal action.

"VR sickness" or "simulator sickness" is a common occurrence that is caused by factors such as a fraction-of-a-second delay in the headset display's responses to the player's movements while using motion-based VR experiences. While its effects are usually temporary, VR sickness can cause disorientation, vomiting, pain and suffering. Perhaps more significantly, VR sickness can occur suddenly; a user might feel perfectly fine while pulling the headset or helmet on and become disoriented within a minute of gameplay.

Could VR sickness be considered negligence on behalf of the hardware and / or content creators, and might it provide sufficient legal basis for a lawsuit that would lead to a verdict in favor of the plaintiff or a settlement payout?

The Court System Lags the Technology, but Existing Legal Principles Apply

While VR technology has been available for decades now, it has only recently begun to reach a mainstream audience, and most judges would likely have little understanding of the context if presented with a lawsuit for injury on the basis of VR sickness.

As in many areas today, progress in VR technology has moved much faster than the law. Nonetheless, traditional legal principles, for example of product liability, would be applied in a VR sickness case. A judge presiding over a VR personal injury lawsuit might not understand the technology or what a VR experience is, but the judge is likely to feel that the same principles that would be applied in a case involving, say, a defective play structure, could be applied. Obviously, this may not always be the case.

. . .

The Potential Effects of VR Sickness Exceed Disorientation

While most VR users do not experience VR sickness, many VR users do, with the degree of sickness varying from user to user. In extreme cases, such users might experience VR sickness that causes vomiting, pain, or injury, which can, in turn, lead to other health problems, medical bills, lost income resulting from absence from work and related losses. It might be argued the company that made the VR hardware in question is negligent for failing to mitigate the risk of VR sickness and as such is liable for the damages and costs that result.

The Potential Costs of a VR Sickness Lawsuit May be High, and the Fine Print is Scant Defense

Were such a suit to be filed against a maker of VR hardware or software, the defendant's counsel might elect to immediately file a motion to dismiss the case on the basis that users are forewarned of the potential for VR sickness somewhere in the lengthy legal terms that accompanied VR devices or content. However, delivery of such verbiage to the user, or the user's "agreement" to these terms, does not automatically provide protection against negligence, nor any guarantee that a judge would dismiss the case. Should VR companies be judged to be selling potentially harmful products to the public, the severity of any alleged sickness, injury, pain, cost, loss of income, etc. might prove to be the deciding factor as to whether the case is heard and the amount of potential damages awarded. And of course if VR sickness is considered sufficiently pervasive for a particular VR platform or content, or combination of both, alleged victims might join as to file a class action lawsuit.

Though some VR companies would be willing and able to finance a prolonged legal battle, undoubtedly some might choose to settle and pay damages to alleged victims to avoid spending time and resources defending the lawsuit or to avoid negative media exposure.

The Best Resolution: Technology

While a large-scale lawsuit alleging VR sickness has yet to arise and the existence and risks of VR sickness are presently not widely known due to the early stage of VR adoption, the growing reach of VR means that it is only a matter of time until this danger is more widely acknowledged and the risk of litigation increases. For these reasons and for the future of this still-young industry, prevention of VR sickness should be a priority for makers of VR platforms and content.

21

INFOGRAPHIC: VR ATTRACTS MORE ATTENTION, BUT AR WILL BE THE WINNER

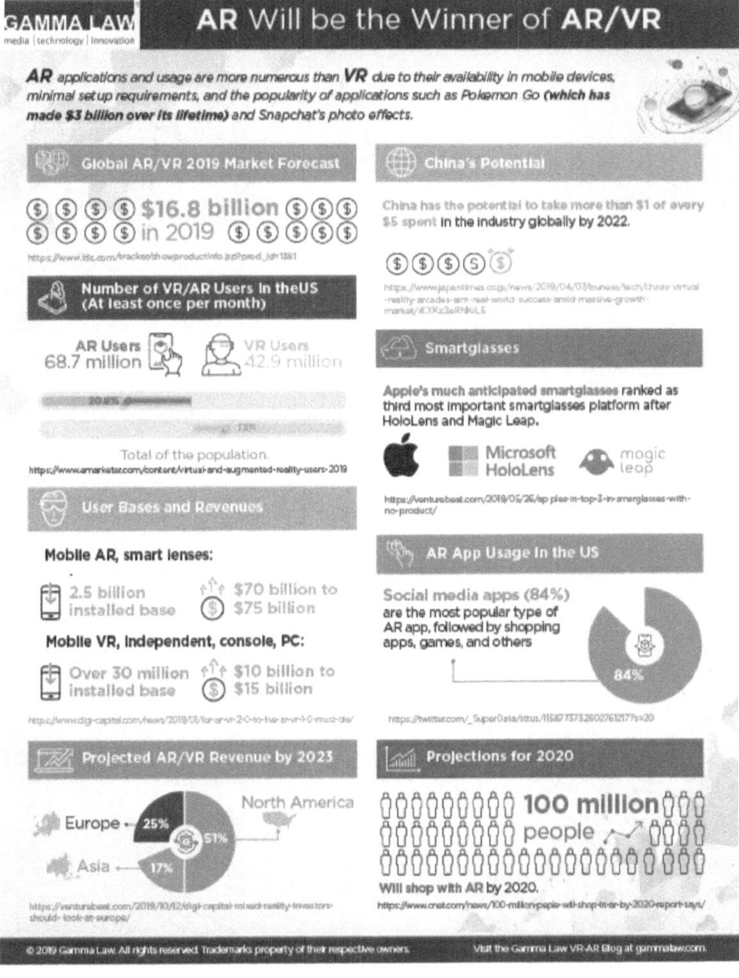

https://gammalaw.com/ar-winner/

BLOCKCHAIN AND CRYPTOCURRENCIES

CLASSIFICATION OF CRYPTOCURRENCIES IS AN IMPORTANT ISSUE

In the US Congress, a newly proposed bill would classify stablecoins (such as the proposed Facebook Libra) as securities. This would provide even more regulation and scrutiny not only to Facebook's new cryptocurrency project, but any other stablecoin already on the market. Outside of stablecoins, the Crypto-Currency Act of 2020 would classify cryptocurrencies into three distinct areas, with each regulated on its own. Crypto-commodities would be regulated by the CFTC, crypto-securities by the SEC, and crypto-currencies by FinCEN. This is by far the clearest proposed guidance for the industry in the United States to date.

The word 'cryptocurrency' is often used to describe any of the myriad of new digital assets available in the market today. This grouping is not inaccurate, but it is highly generalized and fails to capture the different types of cryptocurrencies, the ways in which they are used, and how they should be treated by consumers, businesses, and governments around the world.

While there are numerous ongoing efforts to classify 'cryptocurrencies' based upon asset types and use cases, there is still no general consensus regarding categorizations or naming conventions. The result of this ambiguity is general lack of practical understanding of the different forms of cryptocurrency, both on consumer and governmental levels around the world. As such, the regulatory, legal, and tax requirements and their implications can be very hard to define, which are causes for anxiety and instability in the industry. Classifying cryptocurrencies is a critical step toward bringing wider understanding and stability to this increasingly important asset class.

When is Cryptocurrency not a Currency?

Most people are aware that there is now a multitude of different cryptocurrencies available in the industry, and the perception can be that these are all potentially equally important, or even that they are basically the same thing. However, the range of uses and technical aspects of cryptocurrencies is so broad that it may not be possible to compare any two given cryptocurrencies. This is the case with two of the biggest cryptocurrencies in the industry, Bitcoin and Ether.

Bitcoin is a form of digital cash that is used to make payments across a global network. Ether are 'platform tokens' that are used to power the Ethereum blockchain, a decentralized computing platform. In practice, Bitcoin and Ether are very different, and are not good candidates for direct comparison. Bitcoin should only be compared to other cryptocurrencies intended to perform the same function, and the same applies to Ether. Without understanding of the different asset types and proper classification, inappropriate and illogical comparisons are made between cryptocurrencies with completely different functions.

Categories of Cryptocurrency

The application of categorization allows for cryptocurrencies be appropriately compared and contrasted. Still, there is a variety of ways in which cryptocurrencies might be classified, and there is some disagreement regarding how to categorize some projects that may fall into multiple categories.

The following list of categories is by no means comprehensive, nor are the included classifications agreed throughout the industry, but it offers some insight into the variety of cryptocurrency categories and their differences.

Digital Currencies

The original use case for cryptocurrencies was that of remittances and global payments. Cryptocurrencies could be used to pay for goods and services across borders without incurring significant fees for doing so. Additionally, this type of cryptocurrency would avoid the influence of governments that might seeking to control the flow of money in and out of their economies. This category was first popularized by the illegal drug trade on Darknet sites like Silk Road. However, the usefulness for this type of digital currency soon became obvious, particularly in nations where government-controlled currencies are subject to rapid devaluation and hyperinflation.

Examples: Bitcoin (BTC), Litecoin (LTC), ZCash (ZEC)

Platform Tokens

Platform tokens (also referred to as 'protocol tokens') are used to power entire decentralized networks. These tokens are used to pay for computing power on a network and as economic incentive for operators to keep the networks operating efficiently and securely, and to perform various other functions on the platform. Without platform tokens for economic incentivization, decentralized platforms could be flooded with network requests and entire systems could be brought to a standstill. Many platforms provide a jumping-off point for other projects to create their own utility and/or security tokens directly compatible with the platform upon which they are built.

Examples: Ether (ETH), EOS (EOS), Tezos (XTZ)

Utility Tokens

Tokens that grant the use of a service or utility within a network are referred to as 'utility tokens'. This classification is occasionally used to encompass platform tokens as well. Utility tokens are used for products or services from the company that issues the token, and not for direct investment, although the value of these tokens may rise and fall with demand. These tokens have a real-world application, such as file storage and cloud computing.

Examples: Ripple (XRP), Filecoin (FIL), Golem (GNT)

Security Tokens

Security tokens are cryptocurrencies that under US securities laws are considered to be securities, like stocks or bonds. Security tokens are subject to restrictions under securities laws, and a multi-state public offering will require registration with the US Securities and Exchange Commission. Unlike traditional securities, security tokens have the benefits of decentralized, digital tokens, which include being easily divisible into fractional units and being available for trading globally around the clock.

Examples: tZero (TZROP), CoinMint (CBM), CityBlock Capital (NYCQ)

Regulators will Choose their Own Path

Industry experts and developers may create different classifications or categories for cryptocurrencies, but regulators still have the power to classify these assets in whatever manner they deem fit. How individual governments and regulators will classify cryptocurrencies remains one of the biggest questions in the industry.

Some regulators regard utility tokens as closer to securities, and therefore subject to securities regulation. SEC Chairman Jay Clayton has famously said he has yet to see an ICO that is not a security. At the same time, the SEC has also affirmed that Bitcoin itself is not a security, a fact that many consider to be a major win for the industry.

While cryptocurrencies were created with the intention of remaining outside of government control, categorization by government regulators has significant implications for the freedom and autonomy of cryptocurrencies. The manner in which each project is categorized will determine which governing body is responsible for monitoring, how financial gains will be taxed, and how the cryptocurrency can be used to transact between consumers and businesses.

. . .

Bringing Order to a New Industry

The application of a standardized classification for cryptocurrencies is necessary to further the education of new users, investors, and governmental agencies. It seems likely that the present situation of confusion and disagreement will continue, but the resolution of this issue is an important milestone in the development and maturation of this young industry. The first step, however, must begin with the simple acknowledgement that there is far more to 'cryptocurrency' that simply 'digital cash'.

23

AFTERMATH OF THE ETH CLASSIC 51% ATTACK

Since the publication of the article below, Ethereum Classic has rebounded from the devastating 51% attack. The project's supporters see it becoming even more secure following its Agharta hard fork, which not only bolstered the blockchain's security, but made it fully compatible with Ethereum. However, since the attack on ETC, other cryptocurrencies have shown similar vulnerabilities. The most notable was a 51% attack on Vertcoin, with the attacker re-writing blocks on its blockchain. This was the second such attack to the Vertcoin network in just a few years.

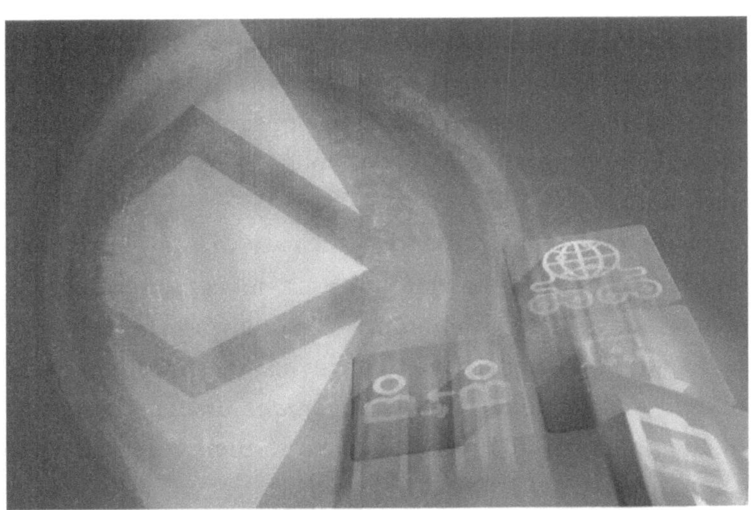

. . .

Fears of a '51% attack' have loomed since the popularization of blockchain technologies. Indeed, attacks were attempted and in some cases succeeded upon some smaller, lesser known cryptocurrencies (see Bitcoin Gold 51% attack), but the scale of the major blockchains rendered them resistant such attacks. That was, until January 7, 2019 when a 51% attack was carried out on Ethereum Classic (ETC).

In the aftermath of the attack, many are speculating how Ethereum Classic might recover from this potentially disastrous incident, but also considering the potential implications for blockchain technology as a whole. The danger of this type of event is by no means limited to smaller blockchains; it is inherent in the very concept of decentralization.

What Happened

On January 7, 2019, an attacker acquired 51% of the total Ethereum Classic blockchain hashing power. This allowed the malicious actor to begin a series of rewrites to the blockchain in an attempt to double-spend the ETC cryptocurrency. Ultimately, the attacker was able to process a series of double-spend transactions on the Ethereum Classic blockchain, generating losses of about $1 million across the network.

Most exchanges responded to news of the attack with announcements stating that they were not compromised, but some, such as Gate.io, announced that they had fallen victim to the attack. The affected exchange businesses lost hundreds of thousands of dollars in covering trader losses and unquantifiable amounts due to the damage to their credibility and reputations.

. . .

An Unavoidable Risk?

As with centralized ledgers, the decentralized nature of blockchains make them susceptible to attack. Anyone who is able to obtain 51% of the hashing power on a blockchain network will automatically gain the power to rewrite previous transactions on the chain, double-spend cryptocurrency, and take advantage of the system. Many, including Litecoin creator Charlie Lee, have stated any decentralized blockchain can experience, no matter the size or stability, can fall prey to a 51% attack.

Accounting for an Attack

The extent to which hashing power can be purchased on the open market is one metric used to evaluate if a coin is susceptible to a 51% attack. NiceHash is the largest marketplace for cryptocurrency hashing power. If the token economics and price work provide an opportunity for would-be attackers to profit, and if there is enough hashing power available for sale on NiceHash, an attack could potentially happen at any time.

Lee described how this played out in the case of the Ethereum Classic attack:

"Be careful w/ coins that are not dominant in their respective mining algorithm, especially ones that are NiceHash-able. ETC has less than 5% of the total Ethash hash rate and is 98% Nice-Hash-able. 1-hr attack costs $5k. Almost $500k has been double spent."

The site Crypto51 provides a live view of most major cryptocurrencies, the amount of money it would cost to conduct a 51% attack, and the percentage of hashing power of the total network available for an attacker to purchase. Using Nice-Hash is not the only way to carry out such an attack, but these metrics can provide key clues to detect a potential blockchain vulnerability.

. . .

Lower Prices Means Easier Attacks

Due to the drops in prices of the entire cryptocurrency market that have occurred over the past year, it is now easier and cheaper than ever to rent the necessary computing power to carry out this type of attack. As mining becomes less profitable, the number of miners on a network falls. Fewer miners means less hashing power, which makes it easier for an attacker to purchase the hashing power required to reach 51% of the entire network.

Reviewing the trend in hash rate of the Ethereum Classic blockchain prior to the attack, the entire network was utilizing half the hash rate that it did at its peak in September of last year. This significantly lowered the financial barrier to carry out the attack.

Source: bitinfocharts.com

Ethereum Classic Price Remains Stable

While conventional wisdom would expect the price to have fallen, this simply wasn't the case. In fact, after dropping only about 10%, the price of ETC stabilized and Ethereum Classic weathered the attack.

There are several potential reasons for this. First, the immediate reaction of many exchanges was to freeze trading on the cryptocurrency, which forced ETC investors to hold through the event and would have prevented a large-scale 'run' on the crypto coin. For instance, Coinbase, one the world's largest crypto exchanges, suspended ETC trading following the attack, rendering users unable to access their ETC funds.

In addition, in spite of the attack, the core development and advocacy team of Ethereum Classic showed no sign of wavering or move to sell their ETC. These core members hold a significant stake in the cryptocurrency, and their demonstrated continued belief in the tokens could well have contributed to stabilizing the price. When asked about ETC price stability after the attack, Castle Island Ventures partner Nic Carter responded, "The truth is that a lot of these assets have dogmatic diehard communities that refuse to submit, and most tokens are held by them anyway."

The Wider and Future Implications

While Ethereum Classic continues to recover from the attack, the shockwaves and implications continue to be felt throughout the cryptocurrency industry. While the advantages of blockchain technology and decentralization have been highly touted, the ETC attack highlighted one manner in which blockchains can be vulnerable to attack and stoked fears of similar attacks occurring in the future.

Blockchain networks are successful because the majority of verifiers (miners and nodes) act in a trustworthy manner. When untrustworthy actors pursue their individual interests at the expense of others, the entire network can break down. The majority of cryptocurrencies will not achieve the 'escape velocity' required to reach a scale that renders 51% attacks impractical, and in these cases, for now at least, we must depend upon collective efforts to act with integrity and pursue the positive progress of this still young and developing industry.

24

FIVE IMPORTANT NAMES IN BLOCKCHAIN
THAT YOU MAY NOT KNOW

2019 was a good year for Bitcoin developer Cory Fields. After discovering a critical vulnerability in the Bitcoin Cash code, Fields spoke about how Bitcoin is also vulnerable to bugs in its system. "The most likely sudden death scenario for a cryptocurrency like Bitcoin is an accidental bug that gets introduced internal to the system", *noted Fields. By going public with his findings, along with his work at the MIT Digital Currency Initiative, Fields has become a household name for anyone who cares about the further development of Bitcoin.*

2019 was also a big year for journalist and cryptocurrency podcaster Laura Shin. In her first live podcast, Shin hosted Ethereum founder Vitalik Buterin who admitted on-air that he fully expected Ethereum to begin falling behind its competitors. She has also garnered a wide range of guests on her podcast Unchained, including Former CFTC chairman Christopher Giancarlo and US Congressman Patrick McHenry, among others. Shin recently passed 116,000 followers on Twitter and has established herself as the go-to name in cryptocurrency media.

* * *

On the topic of 'big names in blockchain', the first names to come to mind are likely those of Bitcoin creator Satoshi Nakamoto, Ethereum founder Vitalik Buterin, and the father of smart contracts Nick Szabo. Yet, there are many important players in the industry who go largely unnoticed for reasons that range from deliberately maintaining a low profile (apologies, Roger Ver) to simply not getting the recognition and credit that they deserve.

The following names are set to support and grow blockchain and cryptocurrency for decades to come even more than the aforementioned figureheads of the industry. These individuals lead not only through technical innovation but also by increasing the awareness of the general public of these revolutionary new ideas.

Ryan Selkis

Lack of transparency is damaging blockchain companies. Without proper regulation, investors and users have little visibility as to whether blockchain networks and startups are acting in a prudent and financially viable manner. In fact, the majority of ICOs and blockchain-based companies are considered to be fraudulent by the general public. Ryan Selkis and his company Messari are doing their best to change this narrative.

At Messari, Selkis has developed a platform on which blockchain companies can provide transparency to investors, regulators, and the general public. His company builds data tools that can enable everyone in the industry to make informed decisions.

Selkis has a robust resume, which includes time on the founding teams at CoinDesk and Digital Currency Group, as well as being heavily involved with Joseph Lubin's brainchild, ConsenSys.

Cory Fields

Ironically, the Bitcoin Core developer is a savior to the entire community of its competitor, Bitcoin Cash. In 2018

Fields anonymously disclosed a vulnerability to Bitcoin Cash which, if left unchecked, could have meant the end of the cryptocurrency as we know it. Not only did Fields apply considerable skills and knowledge in this encounter, but he also brought to light the need for collaboration between blockchain projects, even those seen as threats to one another.

In a post that followed the incident, Fields notes the conundrum he encountered on whether to report the bug in the first place. "I began to question whether it was worth the trouble at all," recalls Fields. "I had no obligation to report anything, after all. But if someone had discovered an equally nasty bug in Bitcoin Core, I would hope that person would bring it to our attention as discreetly and securely as possible. So I decided to do exactly that: create the report I would want to read and deliver it as I would want to receive it."

These days, Fields works at the Digital Currency Initiative at the MIT Media Lab where he helps to develop and maintain Bitcoin Core.

Laura Shin

Laura Shin is active on a variety of forms of media and plays a powerful role in educating and informing the general public on the latest in the blockchain space. Shin previously worked at the media giant CBS and also freelanced for major technology and finance publications, including the Wall Street Journal, Fortune, and ZDNet.

Her work in blockchain began four years ago as a columnist at Forbes where she was tasked with covering the entire cryptocurrency and blockchain industry. While she continues to write for Forbes, Shin has also developed two podcasts, Unconfirmed and Unchained, both of which are big hits across the sector. Every week, Shin brings on industry experts, analysts, and thought leaders to discuss the most important aspects of blockchain and how it is affecting the world. Shin's ability to attract the top crypto names and create a platform for them to share their knowledge with the world make her a significant and positive force in the industry.

Emin Gün Sirer

The Turkish-born Sirer is a computer scientist who has made significant contributions to the fields of computer networking, peer-to-peer systems, and operating systems. Sirer applies his expertise working deep in the underbelly of blockchains, attempting to build scalable solutions for Bitcoin and other networks.

His company, Bloxroute Labs, is comprised of developers and cryptography professionals who utilize the latest in encryption and cryptography techniques to propagate blocks faster on all blockchains, significantly improving transaction times. Sirer was also part of the team which invented Falcon Relay, a method to increase speed on the Bitcoin blockchain by increasing network efficiency and reducing latency between miners.

Sirer is currently the co-director at the Initiative for Cryptocurrencies and Contracts, an organization of academic professionals working to build new cryptographic protocols in the industry.

Peter Van Valkenburg

Van Valkenburgh is likely best known for his appearance last year in front of Congress where he attempted to explain the inner working of blockchain technology to the Senate Banking Committee, all the while battling the pessimistic viewpoints of economist Nouriel Roubini.

Van Valkenburgh is remarkable in his ability to explain

blockchain to the uninitiated with humor, grace, and authority. This outreach is extremely important in the face of government regulators with little to no knowledge on the subject. If Van Valkenburgh can spread blockchain knowledge to those in positions of power, it will go a long way to paving the industry's road to success.

Van Valkenburgh's contributions to the industry go beyond public advocacy: he also is a board member at the ZCash Foundation and the Director of Research at the nonprofit cryptocurrency research institution Coin Center.

Bonus Names: Luis Cuende

Decentralized autonomous organizations (DAOs) are forging a new paradigm when it comes to creating and building organizations. Luis Cuende and Aragon are leading the charge in providing the best resources to make DAOs the new, global organizational standard.

Aragon has the potential to completely revolutionize the way that organizations and businesses function. According to the company, it allows users to, "freely organize and collaborate without borders or intermediaries. Create global, bureaucracy-free organizations, companies, and communities."

Still only 23 years of age, Cuende has already been lauded for his accomplishments and skills many times. This includes being listed as the youngest member on the Forbes 30 Under 30 Europe list, named as the best programmer in Europe under 18 by HackFwd at the age of 15, and acting as an advisor to the European Commissioner of Digital Agenda.

Important Blockchain Advocates

There are many more advocates at work furthering blockchain than just those whose names regularly feature in the news headlines. Developers like Cory Fields or media pundits like Laura Shin play an extremely important roles in establishing the industry and orienting it for success. These people strive to progress the validity, security, and positive public sentiment of the industry, and deserve to be widely acknowledged for their efforts and contributions.

25

THE BUSINESS OF CRYPTO LENDING

Cryptocurrency lenders have built solid businesses and are now venturing into other parts of the industry. Industry leader BlockFi now provides its users with zero-fee cryptocurrency trading as it attempts to take market share away from other exchanges like Coinbase and Gemini. Celsius, one of the biggest players in the crypto lending market, has originated over $4.25 billion in cryptocurrency loans, generating more than $5 million in interest for its depositors. This makes Celsius the fastest growing lender in the cryptocurrency market.

· · ·

The growth of the cryptocurrency industry created demand for new financial products to support crypto asset classes. The current bear market has spurred this demand, as many speculators who refuse to offload their crypto-assets (in hopes of riding out the down trend until the next market turnaround) require immediate access to capital. At the same time, numerous institutional investors are seeking to access cryptocurrencies in order to hedge current positions or implement new trading algorithms. In response to the demand from these such customers, a new cryptocurrency lending market has emerged.

Two Types of Lending

The first type of crypto lending enables borrowers to secure cryptocurrency using fiat currency as collateral. To date, the major borrowers of this nature have been institutions and hedge funds seeking to speculate on the market or gain additional liquidity for high-frequency trading strategies.

The other type of crypto lending, and the one which has garnered more attention from retail investors, allows borrowers to secure fiat capital in exchange for putting up cryptocurrency as collateral. This is predominantly used by retail investors who have suffered major losses (in some cases, as much as 90% of crypto-assets value) over the past year. These investors may need to access capital in order to pay down debts or expenses, but are reluctant to divest themselves of their crypto-assets. Lenders are able to provide capital resources for investors, while allows them to maintain their cryptocurrency holdings.

Lenders in both situations are providing capital to a market which has, up until recently, been viewed as extremely illiquid.

. . .

How Does Crypto-Backed Lending Work?

Rather than utilizing credit scores like traditional banks, lenders in this business require cryptocurrency as collateral for cash loans. Borrowers post cryptocurrency as collateral and pay back loans in monthly installments. If a loan is paid back successfully, the collateral is released back to the borrower. If the loan defaults, the lender has the right to seize the cryptocurrency held as collateral.

While this is very similar to traditional collateralized loans, there are a few differences. First, crypto loans must be over-collateralized; this means someone looking to borrow $10,000 may need to post $15,000 in cryptocurrency value as collateral in order to secure their loan. While this may seem excessive, most lenders require such over-collateralization because of the extreme volatility of cryptocurrency prices. Because prices fluctuate so frequently, lenders fear cryptocurrency put up as collateral may devalue significantly over time, and therefore not suffice in the case of loan default.

Additionally, many crypto lenders have stipulations which allow them to liquidate the cryptocurrency held in collateral if the price falls below a minimum valuation threshold. This is a failsafe to protect the lender against the possible scenario in which the collateral devalues to the point of worthlessness.

Tax Haven

Cryptocurrency investors who have experienced financial gains from trading face significant exposure to capital gains taxes. One way to mitigate this exposure is by securing cryptocurrency-backed loans. This works because, while the purchase and sale of cryptocurrency are subject to capital gains taxes, borrowing capital against cryptocurrencies is not considered a sale of cryptocurrency, and is therefore not subject to capital gains tax.

This is of major benefit to cryptocurrency investors who seek to sell large amounts of crypto-assets outright. It should be noted that the IRS has yet to provide guidelines on these loans (including, for example, whether interest payments are tax deductible), therefore investors should always consult a tax professional before considering cryptocurrency loans for this purpose.

Anyone Can Become a Lender

Crypto lending does not just provide to access capital for borrowers; it enables cryptocurrency holders to earn interest from depositing their cryptocurrency with a lender or becoming direct lenders themselves.

Some companies that provide interest on cryptocurrency deposits, such as Celsius, do not require any specific lock-up period, and pay-out interest every week. Deposited coins are held in secure, cold storage wallets, waiting to be reclaimed in the event of a withdrawal. Other platforms, such as Nitrogen, are a decentralized marketplace for lending, making it easy for anyone to lend cryptocurrency based upon a set of loan terms verified on the blockchain. Borrowers and lenders set their lending terms on the platform and find a party with which to trade. All loans are secured in smart contracts. This peer-to-peer lending model mimics that of fiat lending services such as Lending Club and Prosper.

Earning interest on deposits and direct, peer-to-peer lending bring the cryptocurrencies one step closer to a full-service financial industry.

The Major Players

Cryptocurrency prices faltered in 2018, but this proved to be a catalyst for growth for the crypto lending market; the number of cryptocurrency startups grew exponentially over the year, as more and more investors sought to obtain capital.

The biggest lender in the market to date appears to be Genesis Capital, which originated $1.1 billion in loans in 2018 alone, and is on track to do even more business in 2019.

Galaxy Digital, led by former Wall Street executive Michael Novogratz, raised $250 million for a crypto lending fund. Novogratz sees this fund as a primary way to bring institutional investment into the industry.

Meanwhile, Celsius Network provided $630 million worth of crypto-loans since the launch of its app in July 2018. Celsius has focused on providing these loans not just to retail investors, but to exchanges and hedge funds as well.

Supplying to a Demand

Crypto lending meets a demand for accessible financing in the cryptocurrency market. The practice enables institutional investors to borrow in order to conduct their high-frequency trading and hedge their current positions, and grants retail investors access to capital while still maintaining the potential upside of the future cryptocurrency market and an advantage to avoid capital gains taxes. At the same time, depositors earn interest which allows them to grow their crypto-assets for doing nothing more than making a deposit. Such lending is providing a win-win for everyone involved, and poised for further growth as the entire cryptocurrency industry matures.

26

LIFE AFTER THE BULL RUN:
THE STATE OF ICOS IN SPRING 2019

The SEC is ramping up its crackdown on ICOs. Kristina Littman was recently appointed as the head of the regulator's cyber unit, targeting fraudulent activity involving ICOs and blockchain. In its most notable crackdown, the SEC sued technology company Kik Interactive for the unregistered sale of securities as part of its $100 million ICO. This has not deterred companies outside the US from launching ICOs to raise funds. Hydra, known as the "Russian Silk Road", is raising $146 million via an ICO for its darknet platform.

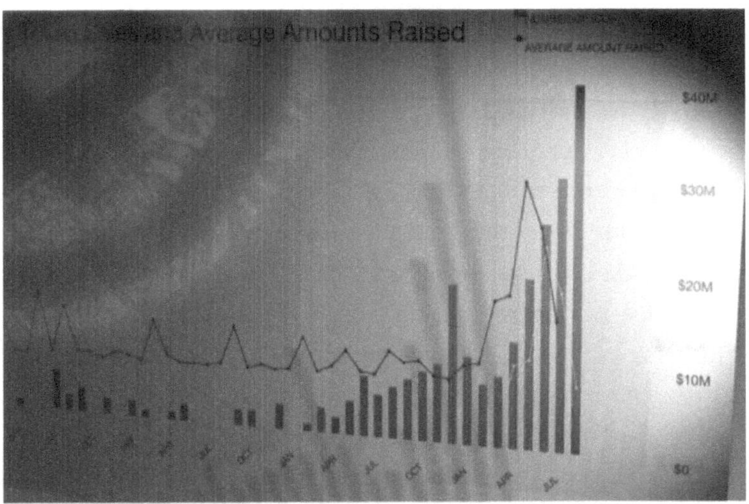

The days of the famed bull market of 2017 are long over. Inflated prices came and went, as did many cryptocurrencies that were not worth their weight in the false promises they made to token holders. As the dust has settled, many have come to believe that ICOs, and many of the scam projects that came along with them, were failures that should never be revisited. But what is the real state of ICOs now that the market has come back down to earth?

ICOs Then and Now

While cryptocurrency market prices dropped drastically over 2018, the number of ICOs did not. According to ICOdata.io, ICOs raised a total of about $6.2 billion in 2017, compared to $7.9 billion in 2018 (note that total fundraising numbers vary from source to source). However, June through December 2018 showed a continuing decline in fundraising by new cryptocurrencies, with less than $500 million raised per month.

Industry Consolidation

As many experts have noted, the demise of the crypto bull run was not just a necessary evil for the industry, but actually a welcome development to those working on long-term projects. As funding dried up, so did those seeking to take advantage of the regulation-free, wild-west of an industry. This is to say, it was clear that much of the boom in ICO fundraising was a direct result of projects that sought to intentionally mislead or even outright defraud token holders.

The last two years saw the rise of many high-profile ICOs such as Tezos, Ethereum, Filecoin, and numerous others. These days, there is nary a peep of any well-known, substantial ICOs in the works.

There is still a variety of token sales in the works which

hope to secure significant funding; Mitoshi hopes to build a new, global crypto-lottery, and is aiming to raise $10-$50 million; meanwhile, Multiven plans to compete with Amazon and eBay as a blockchain-based IT marketplace for transacting, and hopes to fund up to 50 million euros. These are examples of ICOs still fighting to be relevant in a market which has calmed significantly.

Has Regulation Scared ICOs?

This catastrophic drop of over 98% in ICO funding is likely in part due to the industry becoming increasingly fearful of regulators. The Securities and Exchange Commission (SEC) has been quick to clamp down on ICOs that it deems should be registered as securities, and the chances of their evaluating any given project has become more likely than ever.

The SEC is now aggressively pursuing token sales it identifies as unregistered securities. Digital assets featured in SEC's publicly announced examination priorities for 2019. In February of this year, the SEC charged Gladius Network with raising $12.7 million in unregistered securities. As Gladius self-reported the matter, the company is set to return the funds to investors without suffering harsh penalties. In November of last year, the Commission took action against two ICOs, CarrierEQ and Paragon Coin, imposing penalties of $250,000 each on these companies.

Most recently, the SEC has released a Framework for 'Investment Contract in which it provides guidance regarding whether an ICO constitutes an investment. In a related statement, the agency said that the Framework is intended as "an analytical tool to help market participants assess whether the federal securities laws apply to the offer, sale, or resale of a particular digital asset."

. . .

ICOs Are So Two Years Ago. STOs Are the Wave of the Future

One way to raise capital via a token sale without the risk of SEC enforcement, of course, is to register the offering with the SEC. One approach is to tokenize ownership in an underlying asset, which could be real estate or stocks, among others, and register the token issuance with the SEC. Known as an STO or "security token offering," this is a sort of middle ground between ICOs and traditional IPO offerings on public markets.

While STOs did not account for a significant amount of 2018's cryptocurrency fundraising, that could change in the coming years as a variety of STO classifications are in the works that could make it easier to offer a security via these digital mediums. The most well-known of these may be the ST-20 Standard token, which is in the process of being compiled by the team at Polymath. There is also two other security token standards, ERC-1404 and ERC-1400, that are based on the Ethereum blockchain.

On the Ropes

With competition from the new category of STOs and active attention from the SEC, it appears that ICOs may have peaked for good. While the capacity of ICOs to generate capital and buzz once made them an extremely important and valuable tool in the evolution of the cryptocurrency industry, they now only carry value for projects that are not selling securities, and therefore not subject to the SEC's regulation. As the SEC continues to lay down the hammer on questionable token sales, it is likely that many projects that would have previously opted to ICO will now take alternative routes to raising capital.

27

WHY AND HOW CRYPTOCURRENCY EXCHANGES ARE ILLEGITIMATELY INFLATING TRADE VOLUMES

One of the leaders in cryptocurrency data, CoinMarketCap, has launched a Liquidity metric in an attempt to combat what it is regarded as artificially inflated trading volumes on exchanges. This metric factors in a number of variables to help determine how liquid trading volume really is on an exchange. Another large cryptocurrency data repository, CoinGecko, has created its own Trust Score, which takes into account not only trading volumes, but website traffic and order book analysis to paint a more holistic picture of an exchange's true business. The fact is that only the top exchanges that produce any sizable trading volume, even if their numbers are inflated.

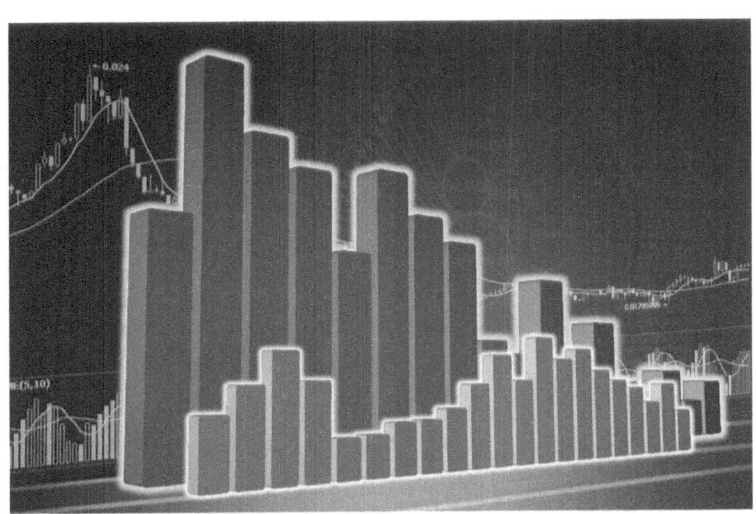

According to CoinMarketCap, daily cryptocurrency trading volumes peaked at over $750 billion per day during the market's bull run, and today regularly exceed $50 billion. These are sizable numbers for an industry that still only makes headlines on the basis of its potential, having yet to establish any significant real-world use cases.

This has prompted investigations into exchange trading volumes, which question if the touted figures are in fact accurate and truthfully reflect the actual volume of business conducted on cryptocurrency exchanges. Unfortunately, the majority of these investigations have concluded that much of the reported volume is falsified, and not indicative of the actual market. In this still largely unregulated industry, exchanges are able to pump trading volume figures in order to appear to be bigger players than they actually are, and so attract more customers to their platforms, increasing their fee revenues.

The Primary Method of Pumping Trade Volumes

One of the most common methods by which exchanges increase their trading volumes is to trade back-and-forth between falsified accounts. This method, known as 'wash trading', occurs when fake accounts are created and trades are conducted between the accounts, generating additional trade volume for the exchange. This method has been used since before cryptocurrencies, and is a concern in all digital financial markets.

Exchanges often use bots to automate this process, never having to conduct the trades directly. Alternatively, trades are conducted between a fake trading account and a colluding broker. This allows a steady flow of trades into the exchange, deceitfully growing the size of the exchange's total volume.

The practice of falsifying volume is of course illegal, but wash trading is alarmingly pervasive in the industry: it was recently estimated that as much as 95% of cryptocurrency trading volumes throughout the industry could be the direct result of wash trading. The Blockchain Transparency Institute was created to provide consumers data regarding how much of an exchange's volume is derived from wash trading. According to the repository, over 90% of the reported volume of exchanges such as OKEx, Bithumb, Bibox, and HitBTC results from wash trading.

Fake Volume Helps Exchanges

There are a number of incentives for exchanges to pump their volumes; probably the biggest motivating factor is to simply user acquisition. According to Binance CEO Changpeng Zhao, this stems from the popularity of crypto ranking sites like CoinMarketCap. "(CoinMarketCap) is [the] highest traffic website in our space, and [the] biggest referrer for all exchanges," explains Zhao in a tweet. "Ranked high on CMC has benefits for getting new users. BUT at the expense of DESTROYING CREDIBILITY with pro users."

A study conducted by crypto-trader Sylvain Ribes found that over $3 billion in daily trading volumes was in fact nonexistent. In addition, Ribes discovered that OKex, one of the largest exchanges in the industry, was the biggest offender.

The Blockchain Transparency Institute found that falsified volumes had led to led to increased fee revenues for the exchanges. The firm's report in December highlighted $100 million in additional fees generated over 2018 as a result of wash trading on crypto exchanges.

While falsifying trading volumes is illegal, unless exchanges feel that there is a real danger of legal action there is little incentive for them to stop the practice of falsely padding volumes in order to increase revenue.

. . .

Exchanges Face Legal Action

While the practice of wash trading has gone almost entirely unchecked to date, regulators are now beginning to catch up. South Korean exchange Komid was caught faking trade volumes in order to deceive investors, which led to the company's CEO receiving a three-year jail sentence. The company was reportedly caught creating fake accounts on its exchange and then using bots to generate false trades to pump up volumes.

Bittrex's application to become a US-based exchange operator was recently denied after the New York Department of Federal Services discovered that the exchange was not following AML and KYC legal requirements to vet customers, and some customers were trading under fake names that included 'Donald Duck' and 'Elvis'. "Bittrex's customer identification program, know your customer, and customer due diligence are seriously deficient as evidenced by the findings of the Department's examiners during their review of sample transactions," stated a note by the regulator.

While cases as extreme as that of Komid are rare, we can expect to see more cases of legal action being taken against exchanges that attempt to deceive investors and generate additional trading fees.

Lack of Regulation is Still a Problem

The primary reason that so many exchanges get away with falsifying volumes and wash trading is the current lack of local and global regulation. In the United States, the Securities and Exchange Commission recently reintroduced the Token Taxonomy Act, which disqualifies cryptocurrencies from being classified as a security. However, the bill does not yet lay out regulations and security measures to ensure that exchanges and other industry players act in accordance with its mandates.

While the US is focused on unraveling and addressing regulatory disorder, other countries are taking steps to ensure that exchanges operate in a fair manner from the outset. In March of this year, the Canadian Securities Administrators (CSA) released a paper highlighting its stance on cryptocurrency trading platforms. In it, the regulators direct exchanges to clarify whether trades classify as futures or derivatives contracts while stipulating that non-security tokens may still be considered derivatives and are therefore subject to regulation.

Take Volumes with a Pinch of Salt

In view of the existence and sheer magnitude of the volume inflation issue, it is little wonder that so much of the financial world is skeptical or even derisive of cryptocurrencies. For all the hype generated by this new technology, its exchange infrastructure cannot be taken seriously. Exchanges are a critical part of any financial ecosystem and important to industry growth and liquidity. If the cryptocurrency industry wishes to be viewed as a legitimate player in global financial markets, it must find a way to eradicate blatantly falsified trading volumes and ensure that exchanges operate with transparency and fairness.

28

BLOCKCHAIN: WHAT HAVE YOU
DONE FOR ME LATELY?

From the outside, it might appear that blockchain has yet to make any real progress. Bitcoin remains an underused digital asset and blockchain solutions have not yet made their way to big businesses. However, a significant amount of development has pushed blockchain solutions forward. "The people who have been focused on blockchain from the beginning — not as a savior but as a technology — are now focused on the practical applications of the technology," saud Devirag Barta, SVP at Mastercard Labs. There are projects working to make blockchain easier for businesses, while companies like Anthem have already announced plans to shift into blockchain solutions in the coming years. Additionally, in late 2019, China announced its support of blockchain technology.

Possibilities and potential can get one a long way in the business world, but at some point, that must give way to real-world results. This balance between excitement over potential and real-world accomplishment may have never been more delicate than in the blockchain industry.

Today, hundreds of blockchain-based projects and companies over almost every industry carry the potential to change the ways in which we transact and conduct business across the globe. Some of these projects are starting to produce real results, while others, including some of the industry's biggest names, still only hold value by virtue of their potential and have yet to live up to expectations.

Bitcoin Has Yet to Make a Real Impact

The most well-known cryptocurrency, Bitcoin, has yet to attain the global adoption its advocates have been predicting. In fact, the majority of all Bitcoin transactions are not for the result of commercial transactions or storing of wealth, but rather speculators trading on exchanges. Heavy trading in Bitcoin is a far cry from the long-term potential applications that form the basis of its valuation such as a replacing fiat currencies for purchasing and salaries and creating new jobs.

What's more, the continuing tribal mentality in the Bitcoin world seems to have worsened. The Bitcoin hard fork that created Bitcoin Cash was followed by another hard fork, which created Bitcoin SV. This immediately led to a battle for hash power between Bitcoin Cash and SV which still rages on today. The factions of Bitcoin are at war, and at present there is no end in sight.

Yes, Bitcoin still has the potential to be the de facto mainstream, decentralized, global currency. Unfortunately, it lacks the required value and ease-of-use for consumers and businesses to take it up on a mass scale. Many hope that scalability projects like the Lightning Network will help increase usage and adoption, but as it stands today, these are still only hopes and not reality.

Ethereum Isn't Faring Any Better

Ethereum, another of the industry's other high-profile cryptocurrencies, has similarly been unable to achieve any sort of mass adoption to date. Touted as the new decentralized internet, Ethereum has almost no working decentralized applications, while the ones that are in operation are severely lacking in users. Applications with the highest number of users are currently cryptocurrency exchanges, games, or gambling applications. At most, these applications have 2,500 daily active users, a figure which is laughably small for a project currently valued at over $17 billion.

There is a great deal of hype around Ethereum 2.0, which is set to move the blockchain from proof-of-work to proof-of-stake in an attempt to solve its scalability problems. However, whether this will lead to wider adoption of the blockchain is unclear. For now, Ethereum still lags behind in its usability and applications.

Gambling and Gaming are First Movers

While arguably not the most meaningful industries for disruption, both gambling and gaming are proving to be the areas in which blockchain solutions are starting to gain traction.

Fraud has a long-time problem in the gambling industry due to a lack of adequate transparency. Blockchains are solving this with provably fair games from lotteries to online poker. For gamblers, transparent and provably fair gambling is a significantly more attractive alternative to relying upon a third-party to ensure security and fair gaming. There are already a variety of blockchain-based casinos and gambling avenues on the market, with many more on the way.

Online gaming is another sector which blockchains have found early success. Gaming was one of the first industries to utilize digital currencies before the proliferation of blockchains, and it is now benefiting from the practice. Popular games like World of Warcraft have their own currency which players can use to purchase in-game items. Implementing blockchain technology on these platforms makes it easier for developers to create and monetize digital goods, and create trustworthy channels for gamers to trade and sell their goods at any time.

Following the success of CryptoKitties, there have been a variety of virtual games that similarly make use of blockchain networks. In addition, games like Decentraland, in which users can build and control virtual worlds, are growing in popularity. Games such as these allow anyone to build and sell their own creations within the game, creating an entire economy within these platforms.

B2B Solutions are Making the Jump

B2B solutions are another area in which blockchains are making headway; distributed ledger technology is finding ways to seamlessly integrate with existing business processes. As Deloitte noted in its recent 2018 Global Blockchain Survey, businesses will begin to put more resources behind blockchain solutions and as a result, "come to better realize how it can improve their business processes and their bottom lines." Of the over 1,000 senior-level executives surveyed, 95% expect their companies to invest in blockchain technology this year, with 65% expecting their companies to invest at least $1 million in the technology over 2019.

In supply chain, businesses are utilizing blockchains to track goods from production to end consumer. One such blockchain solution, VeChain, has already made strides in bringing this concept to market. The blockchain company has partnered with infrastructure giant DNV GL to improve the efficiency of global supply chains and increase transparency of products and suppliers. In the United States, Albertsons, the 2,300-store grocery chain, has started testing product tracking using the IBM Food Trust blockchain platform to help with food safety.

In other news, AT&T announced it would collaborate with IBM and Microsoft to create a suite of blockchain solutions for enterprise customers. The company hopes its solutions will help customers solve complex business problems via an enterprise-grade blockchain environment and trusted cloud platform.

Still a Long Way to Go

The bottom line is that the potential which blockchain advocates have so vocally touted has yet to be realized, and blockchains have yet to prove their worth. However, we are still in the early days of an industry which has much more growing to do. After all, it took over 30 years of development and gradual adoption before the internet hit its stride; one might reasonably expect that the true value of blockchains will come to fruition in a significantly short time period than that, and in some cases in more sudden and disruptive fashion. Time will tell.

29

WHAT LIBRA COULD MEAN FOR THE
CRYPTOCURRENCY INDUSTRY

2019 did not end well for Libra. In October, PayPal, one of the companies handpicked for the Libra Association, backed out of the project. Then, to make matters worse, news came out of Europe that the EU would take a tough stance on the stablecoin. Facebook also has competition from a variety of projects which have announced themselves as direct competitors to Libra. Still, the show must go on and following its September reset, the Libra testnet already had over 50,000 completed transactions as of November 2019.

. . .

Ever since Bitcoin entered the mainstream consciousness, rumors have abounded that major companies would come around to a cryptocurrency mindset and enter the space. Until recently, these rumors amounted to very little, as tech giants eschewed the world of digital assets. This all changed with Facebook's recent announcement of its own cryptocurrency, 'Libra'.

While the announcement has reinvigorated existing cryptocurrency markets and opened the eyes of many to the true potential of digital payments, many cryptocurrency purists are deriding the venture as not only a sham, but detrimental to the original goals of the cryptocurrency community.

Facebook's Libra

Earlier this month, Facebook released a whitepaper outlining its plans for Libra, a new cryptocurrency devised by the social media company. The project is touted as a cryptocurrency for the masses with price stability. Facebook hopes to reach the more than 1.7 billion people around the world who are currently unbanked. Users will not require a Facebook account to use Libra, and the currency will be accepted anywhere Visa or MasterCard are accepted. According to the head of the Libra project, David Marcus, *"Libra's mission is to be a simple, global currency and financial infrastructure that empowers billions of people."*

Libra is backed by real-world assets such as US treasuries and cash deposits, which should help support price stability. It will also use any interest earned from these deposits to maintain low network fees for users.

Libra itself is controlled by companies in the Libra Association, which is comprised of other technology and finance companies including PayPal, Uber, Spotify, Visa, and Mastercard. The company also plans on launching a subsidiary, called Calibra, to manage all Libra data and information separately from that of Facebook.

One of the biggest features of this project concerns digital identity. Facebook hopes to solve the issue of online identity by requiring a decentralized form of digital identification for all users. According to the Libra whitepaper, *"An additional goal of the association is to develop and promote an open identity standard. We believe that decentralized and portable digital identity is a prerequisite to financial inclusion and competition."*

The technology is still in the testing phase, with a public rollout of Libra expected sometime in 2020.

Not Everyone is Positive

While the prospect of a major tech company embracing cryptocurrency has excited many, not everyone is happy. Many of those who celebrate the decentralized, uncensorable nature of blockchain networks and cryptocurrencies feel that Libra should not even be categorized as a cryptocurrency. One reason is that the digital asset will be completely controlled by Facebook and its partner organizations, rendering it subject to censorship and centralization, should these companies choose. This is a marked difference between Libra and decentralized cryptocurrencies like Bitcoin, even though the media tends to group them in the same category.

The development also comes at a time when Facebook is under fire for its questionable privacy practices and concerns are being raised regarding whether it is in breach of antitrust regulations. Michael Pachter, managing director of equity research at Wedbush Securities, said, *"I am not sure that this is the smartest thing for Facebook to be doing, as it will invite further regulatory scrutiny, but it sounds like they're determined to give it a try."*

Some speculate that Facebook is attempting to shape the world of finance to its own world, which will result in social media-like financial system. Others claim Facebook is creating convenience for its users while doing nothing that will benefit the financial system as a whole; think 'PayPal for Facebook'. Even its own partners seem unconvinced of Libra's likelihood of success: many of its 27 other partners signed nonbinding agreements, which do not require that they promote, or even use, the new cryptocurrency.

Who Might be Next?

Now that Facebook has taken the leap into the world of cryptocurrency, other tech companies may well follow suit. Amazon has been rumored to be working on their own cryptocurrency for quite some time. The company previously partnered with Ethereum and Hyperledger on two blockchain-based projects in what seems to be first forays into cryptocurrencies. This makes sense, as Amazon has already made in-roads into financial services, with Amazon Pay and the Amazon Credit Card.

Google's initial response to the popularization of cryptocurrencies was one of extreme skepticism: the company banned all advertisements for cryptocurrencies and related businesses just as ICOs were beginning to take off. The company has since reversed its stance and is now welcoming such technology into its ecosystem. Google already allows Ethereum developers to build applications using Google Cloud services. It is also making it easier for users to view information about their favorite cryptocurrencies. These are only small steps into the cryptocurrency world, but still point to a growing interest by Google.

Google co-founder Sergey Brin even admitted the company has been lagging when it comes to this new technology. *"We probably already failed to be on the bleeding edge,"* he said in reference to blockchain technology.

. . .

A New Beginning, for Better or Worse

Facebook has significant resources, infrastructure, and insights into its user base that it can leverage to bring Libra to market and maximize its chances of success. Libra just might end up being the currency of the future. However, Facebook's trustworthiness has been thrown into question over recent years, a fact that may generate friction as it attempts to onboard millions, if not billions, of users to the company's new digital currency. While the company's stated motive of helping the unbanked is ostensibly well-intentioned, it comes with some strings attached, and those questioning the development do so with no small degree of justification. However, whether it is Facebook or another major tech company that succeeds in popularizing their own digital currency, current developments may likely mark the beginning of a new chapter in the story of the development of cryptocurrencies.

30

HOW BLOCKCHAIN WILL CHANGE
THE MUSIC INDUSTRY

Sony has jumped on the blockchain music bandwagon. The company announced it would use a blockchain-based solution on AWS to manage and protect the rights of digital content creators. Elsewhere, the established cryptocurrency Ripple has created a platform for users to sell their music for XRP tokens. The platform, xSongs, allows musicians keep 100% of the profits from selling a song. The project is still in its beta phase, and is therefore not the easiest to use, but Ripple is moving the needle forward with its new music project.

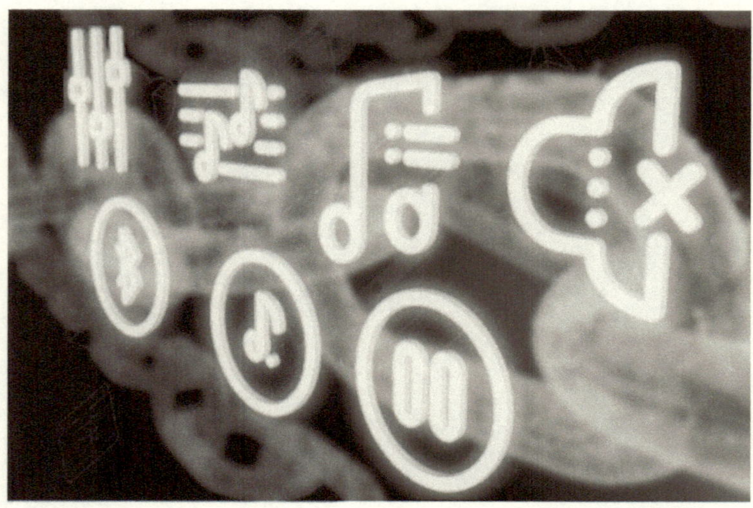

. . .

When Napster released in 1999, the industry was shaken by the new, disruptive technology. Over time, the industry adapted to the new industry dynamics, and the music business today is arguably better for it. The paradigm can be applied to streaming music services like Pandora and Spotify, which form the latest wave of technological disruption to the music industry.

However, the industry is yet in the process of adapting to this change, and many inefficiencies and issues that affect artists and businesses alike remain to be resolved. At present, streaming services routinely underpay artists, refusing to equitably distribute profits in return for their music, and music intellectual property is generally improperly secured or tracked. These are two areas in which blockchain with its immutable ledger and smart contracts that facilitate payments can help to create efficiency and equity in the music industry, as well as ease the transition from dynamic change to stability.

The Issues of Payment and Security

While the proliferation of digital files, smartphones, and streaming music services has served to grow and evolve the music industry, it has also brought new issues, many of which are yet unsolved.

The meteoric rise in size and popularity of streaming services such as Spotify and Pandora belie how little music artists receive as payment. In fact, the disparity between the revenue generated by streaming businesses and the amount that artists are compensated currently presents a significant problem. Spotify recently settled a $1.6 billion lawsuit in which the company was accused of using songs without fairly compensating artists.

Streaming services pay artists very little even in cases of songs that reach millions of people. By some calculations,

Spotify pays an artist between $6,000 and $8,000 for a song that is played one million times, and Pandora pays only $1,650 in the same situation. Additionally, these amounts are not entirely retained by the artist as record labels often take sizable portions. Moreover, there is often significant delay between streaming plays and payment distribution to artists. Artists must often wait weeks or even months to receive royalty payments.

The other major issue is intellectual property. As growth in scale of streaming companies has outpaced the speed of technological advancement, it has become increasingly difficult to keep track of music rights; music rights change hands regularly without any standardization, and IP theft, whether intentional or through negligence, is prevalent.

Fair and Transparent Distribution of Profits

While streaming services earn revenue by delivering vast quantities of music to listeners around the globe, they have also benefited from underpaying artists. Presently, an estimated $2.5 billion in royalty payments that should be paid to artists are delayed or unpaid.

Providing transparency for payments was one of the first applications of blockchain technology, and dates back to the creation of Bitcoin. The principles that govern blockchain payment systems can be applied to create fair and transparent payment systems for the music industry. Bitsong is creating a decentralized music streaming platform in which artists will be compensated directly. Artists utilizing this service are paid for streaming plays by users and can even attach advertisements to their music to obtain more revenue for their music.

Other projects seek to achieve the same outcomes through other means. Musicoin allows independent artists to reach a global audience and receive payment directly by cryptocurrency. Revelator is creating a wallet solution for artists to be paid in cryptocurrency whenever a song is played on radio. Royalty payments are made daily instead of monthly, and smart contracts ensure accurate payment based upon the number of plays.

Solving Intellectual Property Rights

As previously noted, the systems used to manage music rights currently lack transparency and security, and are in need of a major overhaul. Blockchains offer the opportunity to accurately and securely track ownership of music rights. Additionally, rights can be bought and sold with secure payment systems, with all transactions tracked and backed by these blockchain systems.

If management of music rights was simplified and managed in a standardized manner, it would allow anyone to identify the owner of a musical work, and even for rights owners to transfer or sell their rights on the market openly and securely. The Open Music Initiative is one project trying to turn this idea into a reality. By creating an open-sourced protocol, Open Music hopes to bring uniformity to intellectual property rights management in the music industry. The project is comprised of many companies and organizations that participate in the music industry. Mycelia is another project working on this problem and creates blockchain-verified profiles and identification for artists in which digital rights can be stored and transferred. Mycelia combines the concept of blockchain-based digital identities with securing digital property rights.

. . .

Paving the Way to Future Shakeups

Since the launch of the digital age, not so long ago, the music industry has undergone many and significant changes. Digital music files opened the doors to new ways to consume music, and streaming services have pushed the industry even further. The time is now ripe for blockchain technology to fill in the inefficiencies and security gaps prevalent in the music business. By helping secure payments and digital rights, artists and related businesses will benefit from greater transparency and equity across the industry, and provide the foundation for whatever new changes the future will bring.

31

WHAT HAPPENS WHEN THERE ARE NO MORE BITCOIN LEFT TO MINE?

As we approach the next Bitcoin halving (now expected in May, 2020), analysts are questioning how the price of Bitcoin will be effected by its next reduction in mining reward. Some are expecting the price of Bitcoin to reach as high as $50,000 following the halving, noting that a significant drop in supply will create mass demand for the cryptocurrency. Conversely, others believe that this event will have no effect on price, on the basis that the halving is already factored in.

. . .

Bitcoin may be touted by many as the digital currency of the future, but there is a fixed limit to its supply which can never be exceeded or increased. So, what happens when there are no more Bitcoin left to mine, and how will the Bitcoin ecosystem be affected?

The Bitcoin Supply Limit

Traditional currency types have no real supply limit because central banks are able to print more currency at will, as was the case in 2019 when the United States' Federal Reserve Board of Governors gave the go-ahead for the US Treasury to print $206.9 billion in new notes. The amount of dollars printed or destroyed fluctuates from year-to-year based upon a variety of economic factors, thereby changing the amount of physical money in circulation as determined by the central bank.

Bitcoin was designed to be a global, uncensorable currency that was not tied to a central bank or government which could control its supply. As such, the original Bitcoin whitepaper called for production to be decentralized: coins would be minted based on the amount of work done by miners, and not determined by any third-party:

"The steady addition of a constant of amount of new coins is analogous to gold miners expending resources to add gold to circulation."

A supply limit of 21 million coins was set, with no possibility of this limit ever being exceeded or increased, and minting of new coins will become impossible once the supply limit is reached. No one knows why Satoshi Nakamoto, the reputed Bitcoin creator, decided on a fixed supply model. In fact, Nakamoto himself noted in an email that his decision to implement the supply limit was, "an educated guess". It is clear, however, that a capped supply creates a deflationary economic model, a fact of which Nakamoto would have been aware when he made the decision. It is likely that Nakamoto wanted Bitcoin to be unaffected by inflation and increased prices and, by creating a deflationary model, he achieved just that. While estimates differ, it is projected that all 21 million Bitcoin will be mined by the year 2140.

The Future for Bitcoin Miners

Without the Bitcoin reward that miners receive for mining new blocks and keeping the blockchain in consensus and secure, other incentives must be provided for their vital work. Nakamoto had the foresight to consider this, and stipulated that transaction fees will be used as an incentive for miners once the supply limit is reached. From the Bitcoin whitepaper:

"The incentive can also be funded with transaction fees. If the output value of a transaction is less than its input value, the difference is a transaction fee that is added to the incentive value of the block containing the transaction. Once a predetermined number of coins have entered circulation, the incentive can transition entirely to transaction fees and be completely inflation free."

Transaction fees are calculated based on the amount of space the transaction consumes in bytes, which is made of inputs and outputs. When sending Bitcoin, a user is sending not only the currency, but also the entire history of the Bitcoin. This data takes up space, which is known as the 'input' of a transaction. Miners will prioritize transactions with higher inputs which result in a higher transaction fee, unless a sender decides to prioritize their transaction by electing to pay a higher transaction fee.

As the supply of Bitcoin approaches 21 million, it is likely that the ecosystem will vote to increase the block size on the Bitcoin blockchain. Doing so would allow more transactions to be filled into each block, and in turn, create more transaction fees per block for miners. This would keep miners incentivized to secure the network even as the Bitcoin rewards dwindle toward zero.

The Law of Supply and Demand

Provided that Bitcoin is able to retain value and reach mainstream adoption, the 21 million Bitcoin supply limit will dramatically affect the value of Bitcoin. The law of supply and demand dictates that the price of a product or goodwill rise when there is an increase in demand without a subsequent increase in supply. As such, the price of Bitcoin and the overall value of the Bitcoin economy is expected to increase as the supply limit nears.

This value could be driven up even further if Bitcoin is able to overtake gold. Bitcoin's market capitalization is currently in the region of $200 billion, while the world's existing gold supply has a total value of around $8 trillion. Many experts believe that it is only a matter of time before the value of Bitcoin overtakes that of gold. Were this to happen, more investors would be attracted to Bitcoin and the subsequent increase in demand for the supply-constrained digital asset would drive up its price and return current investors significant amounts of money.

The Future of Money Supply?

Unlike fiat currency, the supply of Bitcoin is controlled by transparent and immutable laws and rules. In this way, Bitcoin provides its users with both stability and visibility regarding the supply status of the digital asset, but it also means that its future is, for better or for worse, beyond the control of any single party.

Of all of the questions regarding what will happen with there is no more Bitcoin to be mined, the matter of exactly how transactions and fees will be impacted has to be the among greatest. Transaction fees could rise substantially if there is an increase in volume of transactions. Or, if the block size limit is increased, transaction fees could remain fairly constant, as more fees will be included in a single block for miners, allowing more transactions to be verified in the same amount of time. As time passes, Bitcoin edges closer toward the end of supply; provided that it can survive the journey, arrival at this destination will make or break the cryptocurrency for good.

32

JAPAN: AN UNLIKELY CHAMPION OF BLOCKCHAIN & CRYPTOCURRENCIES

Blockchain development in Japan continues to advance. JPMorgan will launch its own blockchain network in Japan by early 2020, with over 80 domestic banks in the country intent on joining the platform. Private sector Japanese companies are also using blockchain technology. Kansai Electric Power Co, Japan's second largest power utility company, is extending its trial of a renewable energy credit system powered by blockchain. All the while, the country's regulators have allowed for the flow of digital assets to be easy and seamless. The Japan Financial Services Agency (FSA) has approved 21 cryptocurrency exchanges in the country, making it easy for consumers and businesses to trade the assets without questions over legality.

Japan has long been a technology leader, and companies like Honda, Sony, and Nintendo (to name a few) have brought hugely influential technologies to the world, with the active support of the Japanese government. It is therefore perhaps not surprising that blockchain technology has developed significant support in the country, with even the Japanese central bank advocating for its use. The irony is that a country that still places heavy reliance on physical currency has become a world leader in the cryptocurrency and blockchain movement.

A Paper-Cash Economy

Despite the impressive adoption of digital payment methods, through mobile phones and cash cards, Japan is one of the few developed countries where the majority of payments are still made using paper bills or metal coins rather than cashless electronic systems. The economy incurs $18 billion per year in costs associated with moving around physical currency; costs that could be reduced with greater adoption of digital transactions. The move toward digital has begun, however, just at a far slower pace than other similar economies. Prime Minister Shinzo Abe noted that he hopes 40% of the country's payments will be cashless by the year 2025.

The country has one particularly pressing reason to move toward a cashless economy: the upcoming 2020 Olympics in Tokyo. The legion of business and individual visitors from around the world will expect to be able to purchase quickly and easily, without having to worry about paper Yen and exchange rates. Visa is making strides in the push toward digital payments in Japan, but cryptocurrencies are not far behind. Mitsubishi UFJ Financial Group, Japan's third largest bank, is working with US content delivery service Akamai to design a consumer payment system built on a blockchain network. This network is supposed to be able to verify transactions in a matter of seconds, and have a capacity of one million transactions per second. This would be a significant resource for processing of the millions of additional transactions that will be experienced over the 2020 Olympics.

The Japanese Government is Onboard

Government backing is a necessity for any nation to fully embrace blockchain and fortunately the Japanese government seems to be supporting this new technology.

As one example, the Japanese government is working on an alternative to the SWIFT payment system used for international bank transfers. The new system uses a cryptocurrency and blockchain network that is intended to allow for faster cross-border payments. While much about the project is still a mystery, it is seems to be a clear indicator of the optimism that Japan and the Japanese government have for blockchain technology and its future potential.

In June 2018 the government launched a 'blockchain sandbox' as a way to support companies introducing new blockchain ideas and business models. In this digital space, companies can experiment with new technologies such as blockchain without real-world implications. This allows for testing of new ideas without real-world negative consequences and facilitates innovation and progress at a rapid pace.

A senior Bank of Japan official recently told the Nikkei Asian Review that the country's central bank supports blockchain, particularly in comparison to China. In a candid and remarkably supportive statement, the official said *"Because of their fear of capital outflows, the Chinese see every financial asset as the enemy,"* said the official. *"But we don't worry about outflows. We are in love with the technology behind it and we are in touch with the technology community."*

. . .

Large Companies Start Using Blockchain

A number of notable Japanese corporations have begun implementing blockchain networks into their existing businesses. The country's largest e-commerce company, Rakuten, has received permission from the Japan Financial Services Agency (FSA) to begin operation of a cryptocurrency exchange. In mid-2018, Rakuten purchased the cryptocurrency exchange Everybody's Bitcoin for $2.4 million, and the company said *"In order to provide cryptocurrency payment methods smoothly, we believe it is necessary for us to provide a cryptocurrency exchange function, and have been considering entry into the cryptocurrency exchange industry as the Rakuten Group."*

Some of the country's most popular apps are also embracing crypto: LINE, the ubiquitous messaging app with 80 million monthly active users, was approved for a cryptocurrency business license in September. The company plans to design a token economy around its flagship app, similar to those of Telegram and Facebook, to connect users and service providers. There have already been several dApps created in the LINE digital economy, with many more expected to be released over the coming year.

A Preference for XRP

Japanese traders have historically favored XRP over other cryptocurrencies, and the XRP cryptocurrency has been accumulated at a higher rate in Japan than comparable cryptocurrencies. According to reports, 61 of Japan's 200 banks are open to the idea of using XRP in financial transactions. Ripple, the company behind XRP, has even partnered with SBI Holdings, a branch of one of Japan's largest companies, to provide dividend payments to stockholders in the form of XRP tokens.

SBI Remit, a subsidiary of SBI Holdings, has partnered with Siam Commercial Bank to use Ripple's blockchain solution to help users send payments easily between Japan and Thailand. With 47,000 Thai nationals currently living in Japan, this partnership could have significant implications.

Ripple itself has brought its University Blockchain Research Initiative (UBRI) into several academic institutions in Japan, which should further the relationship between the nation and XRP. Ripple seems enthusiastic about the future prospects for cryptocurrency in Japan relative to other countries. *"Japan is quickly becoming a leading force in crypto assets and blockchain. The region has always been forward thinking and exploring ways to improve the current financial system,"* said Emi Yoshikawa, Senior Director of Global Operations at Ripple.

The Wheels are in Motion

Given its still-ongoing adherence to traditional paper money, there may be no developed country more primed to benefit from cryptocurrencies than Japan. The country has seen a huge rise in blockchain technological advancement and cryptocurrency adoption, with its government and many major corporations already on board.

While countries such as the United States remain ambiguous in their stance on blockchain networks, Japan has made it clear that it believes this technology is the wave of the future, and as a pioneer of technological advancement and first-mover in the blockchain industry, the advancements that it makes in this area may eventually benefit the entire world.

33

LET'S BE CLEAR: CHINA BACKS BLOCKCHAIN, NOT BITCOIN

The Chinese legal system is already incorporating blockchain into its court processes. Over 3.1 million litigation activities in China over the current year were settled using blockchain and smart contracts. This could lead the country to adopt AI-powered judges in the future. All told, more than 500 blockchain projects have registered with the government, putting China in the driver's seat as a world leader of blockchain adoption. There is a significant concern that the US could fall behind in this technology, particularly following China's announcement of its ban on the use of US technology by government workers.

The Chinese government has historically been quick to suppress any innovation deemed as troublesome or counter to the stability and administration of the ruling regime. This of course included blockchain technology, which follows and maintains a philosophy of decentralized control, but last week China announced itself to be a blockchain supporter. While China now ostensibly supports blockchain technology, it still apparently holds disdain for cryptocurrencies, which subvert government-backed and centrally-controlled currencies.

The Backstory

For years, China has been adamant that cryptocurrencies and the accompanying blockchain technology are nothing more than fads that attempt to undermine governments. As such, the Chinese government enacted numerous rules and restrictions in an attempt to ban cryptocurrencies and their usage in its country.

ICOs were banned in China in 2017, just at the height of their global boom. Domestic exchanges were shut down, and offshore and foreign exchange platforms were banned. The government has been quick to prosecute ICOs that have attempted to circumvent the bans, and even plans to eliminate Bitcoin mining in the country, which it claims is a waste of resources.

Yet, it should be noted that cash is already almost obsolete in China, as millions of consumers use mobile payment apps like WeChat Pay and Alipay. Therefore, it isn't a stretch to imagine that Chinese consumers might be quick to adopt new, blockchain-based mobile payment solutions and digital currencies if they were given the opportunity.

· · ·

The Announcement

In October this year, Chinese President Xi Jinping spoke publicly about technology and innovation in his country, and highlighted blockchain as one of the areas in which other countries are making innovations, and where China should look to build upon its current technology:

"Major countries are stepping up their efforts to plan the development of blockchain technology. Greater effort should be made to strengthen basic research and boost innovation capacity to help China gain an edge in the theoretical, innovative and industrial aspects of this emerging field."

President Xi called for more investment and research into the technology as the country continues its progression to be a leading financial power. He even went as far as to include blockchain as one of his nation's "core technologies" that will lead it into the future.

Chinese media was quick to pounce on the news. Immediately following the announcement, all anti-blockchain media sentiment in China was erased from existence, and articles referring to blockchain as a scam were banned. Thus began a new era of a blockchain-supporting China.

Bitcoin Prices Spike

The announcement out of China sparked a frenzy of excitement and investment in Bitcoin that drove the price from $7,500 to about $10,500 in just a matter of hours. Other cryptocurrencies, particularly those based in China or with relationships in the country, also saw their prices skyrocket. NEO, often referred to as the 'Chinese Ethereum', increased over 30%, while Tron posted over 20% gains.

Most experts agree that the increases in value in Bitcoin and other cryptocurrencies are only a short-term phenomenon, but prices could continue to rise if China pushes forward with its blockchain plans and investors view this as an endorsement of the entire industry, cryptocurrencies and all.

Misconstrued Information

This short-term spike in the price of Bitcoin is not backed by any evidence that China is supporting the decentralized cryptocurrency. In fact, state-run media in China specifically stated that the Chinese government is against Bitcoin and other cryptocurrencies, and that its support only extends to state-backed cryptocurrencies and blockchains: *"The rise of blockchain technology was accompanied by that of cryptocurrencies, but innovation in blockchain technology does not mean we should speculate in virtual currencies."*

Chinese reporters commented that investors should keep the comments in perspective. *"Innovation in blockchain technology is not equal to speculation in virtual currency. It should be prevented from using blockchain to hype up altcoins and other activities,"* says one reporter.

Still, because of its massive global power and influence, a positive sentiment toward blockchain in China has been viewed as positive sentiment for the entire cryptocurrency industry. *"This is a clear signal that the leader of the world's second-largest economy is moving towards embracing the technology – in which Bitcoin plays a vital part – and therefore taken as a positive boost for the whole digital currencies sector,"* Nigel Green, CEO of financial advisory firm deVere Group, told The Independent.

China's Blockchain Innovations

The most important blockchain project in China remains its state-run cryptocurrency, which is expected to be released in the near future. The cryptocurrency will operate such that both China's central bank, the People's Bank of

China, and its large financial institutions can issue the digital currency. It is expected that the cryptocurrency will reduce costs and decrease time for digital transactions. Concurrently, it will provide the government with greater surveillance and control over the money supply in its country. In diametric contrast to Bitcoin, where users remain anonymous, the Chinese government could eventually have full access to the wallets and financial information of its citizens.

China is moving forward with blockchain-based solutions for public services. A smart city ID system is scheduled to be rolled out this year. The project will assign unique ID codes to cities to monitor smart infrastructure. Blockchain will be used to help standardize and administer the codes in a safe, secure manner. The government is even using a decentralized application (dApp) to have its leaders pledge their allegiance to the Communist Party on the blockchain. These attestations are made public and shareable so that party allegiance can be viewed at any time.

In addition, over 10 million blockchain-based invoices have been issued by the Shenzhen Tax Service, totaling close to $1 billion in value. Over 7,600 companies in the finance, retail, hotel, and other industries have used the Shenzhen e-billing system that is backed by blockchain and developed by the tech giant Tencent.

China Gets the Drop on the US?

The United States government has yet to make a strong commitment to cryptocurrencies and blockchain technology. While many US companies are innovating with these new technologies in useful ways, the US government is doing little to foster such development.

Facebook CEO Mark Zuckerberg warned the US Congress that if the country does not continue to innovate in finance it could easily be superseded by China in the realm of digital payments.

Mike Wasyl, managing partner at fintech strategy firm DeerCreek, sees China, not the United States, as setting the table for the rest of the world. *"China's just making a giant move forward in trying to come out with their central bank digital currency first,"* says Wasyl. *"It'll definitely send messages to the world that this is kind of the new paradigm."*

China has taken the lead with blockchain, and it is unclear whether the United States will step up to the plate and take similar action of their own. For now, China has a head start in the race of blockchain innovation, even if it doesn't view Bitcoin and other cryptocurrencies as viable tools for the digital economy.

INFOGRAPHIC: CRYPTOCURRENCY INDUSTRY SNAPSHOT NOVEMBER 2019

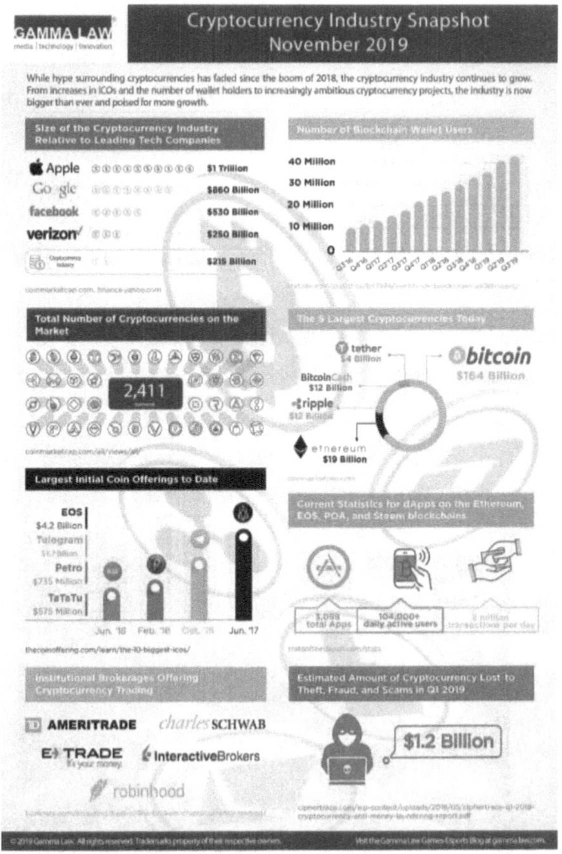

http://gammalaw.com/crypto-11-19/

THE FALL AND RISE OF DAOS

*A*ccording to Ethereum founder Vitalik Buterin, creating governance mechanisms for DAOs remains a top priority to move the cryptocurrency industry forward. "DAOs are cool, but current DAOs are still very primitive; we can do better", stated Buterin. *One DAO driving progress is Stake DAO, a revenue-sharing DAO producing returns for investors willing to stake their PoS cryptocurrencies to the DAO. There is also SingularDTV, which introduced its DAO to fight censorship resistance and give power back to content producers. As a DAO, the system can be attacked or fail and still have the ability to hard fork and move forward without any negative repercussions.*

Bitcoin introduced the world not only to decentralized currency, but also to a new way to organize and operate large scale projects. As an open-sourced, decentralized protocol that is not owned or operated by any single entity, Bitcoin provided a new paradigm that could be extended and applied to actual organizations. This model of organizations that are sustained and run by networks of participants is now being proliferating and developing, creating a new ecosystem of organizations for the global, digital age.

What is a DAO?

For over two hundred years, corporations have been the most popular structure for companies to take. In this model, owners, employees, and customers form a hierarchy in which owners hold ultimate decision-making power within the organization. However, the advent of smart contracts and blockchain technology has paved the way for new manners in which to organize and grow businesses.

A DAO (Decentralized Autonomous Organization) is an organization that has no centralized ownership or hierarchy, and is operated by a decentralized base of stakeholders which can include customers, employees, shareholders, and others. Rather than applying management by humans, a DAO operates under laws of code which are open for all stakeholders to review and monitor. Decisions within a DAO are made not in a hierarchical structure, but instead by democratic voting.

The DAO Debacle

The first DAO achieved renown not because of its success, but because of its epic failure. In 2016, a decentralized organization was created for the purpose of investing in cryptocurrency projects. This DAO would collect funds from investors, pool those funds together, and allow DAO token holders to submit proposals to fund projects. Known simply as, "The DAO", this organization operated on the Ethereum blockchain and at the time raised around $150 million in Ether tokens.

A mechanism within The DAO was implemented to ensure that minority holders could not be taken advantage of by the majority: minority holders were able to retrieve their funds if they voted to reject a proposal but that proposal still went on to be funded. Unfortunately, a malicious actor discovered a way to utilize this function to retrieve funds many times over before The DAO became aware of the deceit. Ultimately, the attacker made off with 3.6 million Ether.

The damage was not limited to the loss of Ether. Following the attack, the Ethereum blockchain was split in a hard fork in order to roll back the stolen funds and return them to The DAO investors. The split caused a deep schism in the Ethereum community: some Ethereum stakeholders challenged the idea of rolling-back the blockchain, taking the position that code should be immutable and never subject to revision. These stakeholders went on to adhere to the original Ethereum blockchain and rebranded themselves Ethereum Classic.

Rising from the Ashes

Following the debacle of The DAO, skepticism about this new type of organizational structure ran high among the media and general public. However, many developers and industry experts still saw potential in the concept, and contributed to building the support infrastructure required for DAOs to operate effectively. Today, many projects are in progress to deliver such infrastructure and educate the public on what DAOs are able to accomplish. The common overarching goal is to allow anyone to create their own DAO without any technical knowledge or background.

Aragon is creating a suite of tools for the creation and management of DAOs. The project operates as a DAO itself, a testament to its commitment to the new space. While the project is still in its early stages, key functionalities, such as a voting mechanism, funding, and payroll, are already available. DAO stack is a similar project which acts as an operating system for decentralized organizations; it allows for seamless collaboration between DAO participants and facilitates the management of workflows and processes.

Other decentralized services exist to enable DAOs to operate in a fully decentralized manner. Programs such as Gitcoin allow organizations to decentralize the bounty process, which is extremely helpful in the world of development; file storage services such as IPFS encrypt and distribute pieces of files around the globe; decentralized lending platforms such as DeFi or MakerDAO provide loans which can be collateralized by cryptocurrencies in order for investors to finance new DAOs.

Current Notable DAOs

Today, increasing numbers of projects and organizations are adopting this organizational method. Ethereum is one notable example: while Ethereum founder Vitalik Buterin remains a prominent figurehead of the crypto asset, the project actually operates as a DAO, with no centralized control for the project's operations. In fact, most major cryptocurrencies operate as DAOs, adhering to the tenet of decentralization that made blockchain technology so intriguing in the first place.

In fact, a wide variety of projects are embracing this new

paradigm. Fundraising DAOs, backed in some cases by venture capital and in some cases by crowdfunding, are now shaping the future of fundraising. For example, Giveth is an open-source charitable giving DAO, and the Daox protocol helps organizations fund their projects, and gives investors voting rights in their investments.

Another area currently gaining traction is decentralized prediction markets which do not rely upon any singular point of failure or entity to attest to outcomes. In this model, users create prediction markets to wager on outcomes of specific events. When an event concludes, winners are paid via smart contracts. If the outcome of the event is in question, a user may challenge the outcome, following which a decentralized network of participants verifies the correct outcome.

Augur is the biggest name in this space, and allows anyone to create their own prediction market and/or wager on outcomes on everything from sports to weather to political predictions.

A New Type of Organization

While the concept of a decentralized organization is still foreign and in some cases even incredible to many, it is possible if not likely that the corporation may one day be supplanted by other, better ways to operate businesses and projects, and DAOs may be one. Even now, the wisdom and long-term viability of the corporation is in question; in addition to ethical and environmental concerns, some of the world's biggest companies have so much power that they have major political influence, and some are considered by some to be in violation of antitrust laws.

After 200 years of social, technological, and organizational evolution, the world may be ready for a new type of organization: one which aligns all stakeholders in a democratized fashion so that no single entity can inequitably exert its power or control over others. Doing so will bridge the gap between those in power and give that power back to the people. Many proponents of DAOs believe that the next evolution of business is here, and it is decentralized.

ABOUT GAMMA LAW

Gamma Law is a San Francisco-based firm supporting select clients in cutting-edge business sectors. The Firm provides clients with the support required to succeed in complex and dynamic business environments, push the boundaries of innovation, and achieve their business objectives, both in the United States and internationally.

Website: www.gammalaw.com
Email: info@gammalaw.com
Phone: +1 (415) 901-0510

Twitter: @GammaLaw
Facebook: https://www.facebook.com/GammaLaw/
LinkedIn: http://www.linkedin.com/company/gamma-law/

www.ingramcontent.com/pod-product-compliance
Lightning Source LLC
Chambersburg PA
CBHW031307160726
47993CB00001B/322